New
Ways with
POLYMER CLAY

Other Books
Available from Krause Publications

Beautiful Beads,
by Alexandra Kidd

The Crafter's Guide to Glues,
by Tammy Young

Dazzle: Creating Artistic Jewelry
and Distinctive Accessories
by Linda Fry Kenzle

Exotic Beads,
by Sara Withers

Fanciful Frames,
by Juliet Bawden

Papier Mâché Style,
by Alex MacCormick

New Ways with POLYMER CLAY

The Next Generation of Projects and Techniques

KRIS RICHARDS

Published by Krause Publications
Iola, Wisconsin

All Rights Reserved
Published by Krause Publications
    Iola, Wisconsin 54990

Cover and Interior design by
Green Graphics/Stan Green

Cover photos by Donna Chiarelli

Illustrations by the author

Interior photography by
David Savage, Savage Photography

Manufactured in the United States of America

Library of Congress Cataloging-in-Publication Data
Richards, Kris.
    New ways with polymer clay : the new generation
of projects and techniques / Kris Richards.
       p.   cm.
    Includes index.
    ISBN 0-8019-8869-1
    1. Polymer clay craft. I. Title.
TT297.R53   1997
731.4'2—dc20   96-42125
                                            CIP

    4 5 6 7 8 9 0   6 5 4 3 2 1 0

The following are registered trademark names that appear
in this book: *AMACO Friendly Cutters, AMACO's Friendly
Plastic Arts and Crafts GOOP, Bic Round Stic pen, Black and
Decker Handy Choppers, Carnival Arts Ultraglaze, Cernit,
Chi-Chi's salsa jar, Craftsman's Goop, Creatively Yours Super
Glue from Loctite, Daubing Paste, D&CC (Decorator & Craft
Corporation), Delta Ceramcoat Artist's Acrylic Paint, Dremel
Mototool, Elmer's, Enjoyment Products, E 6000, FISKARS
Paper Edgers, FIMO, Foredom polisher/buffer, Friendly Clay,
Granitex, Hamilton Beach, Johnson's paste wax, Kemper
tools/pattern cutters, Krylon's matte spray coating, Leather
Factory, Lexan, Loctite liquid super glue, Lucite, M&M's,
Masonite, Mix Quick Kneading Medium, Plexiglas, PROMAT,
Pyrex, Loctite Quick Tite super glue, Rub 'n Buff, Sanford
Sharpie Extra Fine Point marker, Sculpey/Polyform, Sculpey III,
Sobo Premuim craft and fabric glue, Solid Diluent, Super
Elasticlay, Tacky Glue, Wilton cookie or canapé cutters,
X-ACTO knife.*

*T*o my husband, Gary. I am so proud of you, me, us! We have come full circle. Even though it took us over twenty-four years to get there, look what we have achieved! We're both pursuing our long-sought dreams.

I shudder to think what my life might have been had I never met you. You are my love, my best friend, my lifetime hero. You guide and nurture, allowing me to learn through my failures and successes. You keep me complete, secure, and safe. You've allowed me the freedom to choose my own path, somehow never doubting my abilities, even when I do. No matter what I try, what heartaches I unearth, you're always there for me. You keep me buoyed, yet grounded. This is not my book, it is our book.

To my daughter, Nicole, who was the hand model for the drawings in this book. Besides having lovely hands, you have a lovely heart. Although it took many hours of your time, during that time in your life that being with Mom (for most teenagers) is a grueling experience, you did your very important "job" willingly and (for the most part) without complaint. We laughed and joked and grew closer. We make a great team, you and I! Can I be the artist for *your* book? I love ya, kid, you make me proud.

CONTENTS

Acknowledgments ix

Introduction x

PART ONE: POLYMER CLAY BASICS

CHAPTER ONE
Polymer Clay Brands: Which One to Choose? 2
A Survey of the Clays.. 3
    Cernit — 3
    FIMO — 5
    Friendly Clay — 11
    Granitex — 13
    PROMAT — 13
    Sculpey III — 14
    Sculpey/Polyform — 15
    Super Sculpey — 16

CHAPTER TWO
Working with the Clays 18
General Work Surface Guidelines............................. 18
Successfully Lighting Your Work Area 19
Good Posture.. 19
Tool Time 20
    Customizing Kemper Cutters — 21
    Nontraditional Tools — 21
    Power Tools — 22

CHAPTER THREE
Starts to Finishes.. 23
Adding Textures, Colors, and Shapes 23
    Textures — 23
    Colors — 26
    Shapes — 26
Imitation: The Best Form of Flattery....................... 28
General Rules for Baking Polymer Clay 28
    What to Bake On — 28
    Which Glues to Use — 30

The Definition of Finish 32
    Added Finishes — *32*

Clean-Up and Storage 33
    Cleaning Your Pasta Machine — *34*
    Storing Your Polymer Clay — *35*

CHAPTER FOUR
Working with Color 36
    Marbleizing 36
    Color Mixing 36
        Full-Color Mixing Methods — *38*

PART TWO: POLYMER CLAY PROJECTS

Projects 42
    Chocolate Sweets for the Dieter 42
    Grandma's Old-Fashioned "No-Cal" Sugar Cookies 44
        Angels, Stars, Teddy Bears, and Christmas Trees — *47*

    The Internet Ink Pen 48
    "Spicy" Jar Lids 52
        Mexican Sombrero Lid — *53*
        Red-Flowered Lid — *55*

    Gilded Antique Frame 56
    Springtime Birdhouse Ornament 60
    Good Morning, Glory! Garden Soap Dish 66
    Christmas Package Frame 72
    Recycled Santa Lightbulb Ornament 77
    Christmas Tree Box 82

Resources 89

Index 95

ACKNOWLEDGMENTS

An artist has so many people, friends and family, who share in her growth and achievements, but there are many who go above and beyond what is expected. These special people are part of a beginning, the creation of who the artist is, what paths she follows, and how she grows. The Mom who encourages her child with words of encouragement, a smile and a hug when the first colorful crayon scribbles are given as a proud gift. Later, during the years that are so critical to an artist's fine-tuning and spiritual growth (the "terrible teens"), there are teachers, friends, and family who nurture her. The young college entrepeneur, striking out into a big world with even bigger bravada with cherished friends and fellow artists to support her. Later, a husband who understands and helps her during those late-night crazies, deadlines, even when he may not see her for hours on end, during those wildly creative streaks. Families who don't have to be asked to "pitch in" to pick up the void left by the artist's latest project. Daughters who manage to maintain their high scholastic standards and manage to bring home all A's, even when all they see of their mother for hours on end is the back of her head at the computer! Family members who support you, even though they don't really understand *why* you are driven to create, write, travel, teach, and be away from them far too often. Friends who say the right thing to soothe bruised egos, tell a funny joke or two, and give a reassuring note of encouragement, a hug, and a smile.

I am the lucky one. I have all this. In addition, I have a support network in the creative industry that is second to none—people who not only encourage me by sending me their latest color or brand of clay or the latest support product or craft material, but who generously send however much I need, whenever I need it. Presidents and CEOs of companies who are my friends, who share their expertise and who are never too busy to speak to me or to return my call as soon as they can. Artist friends, professionals, who lend me their expertise, knowledge, and ideas with grace and confidence. My deepest most sincere gratitude goes to you all. Through you, I have found the talent that lies within, the love to express it and the courage to use it.

Sincerest thanks to: The folks at the American Art Clay Company (AMACO)—Nancy Elliot, Ed Walsh, Mark Lee, and Maureen Carlson (my hero!)—for encouragement, friendship, inspiration, support, and generous donations of Friendly Clay, Rub 'n Buff, FIMO, push molds, and Friendly Cutters); Clay Factory of Escondido (Marie and Howard Segal) for their advice and friendship; Decorator & Craft Corporation (Fleeta Jennings for her generosity and help with the papier-mâché items); Delta Technical Coatings, Inc. (Sobo glue and Ceramcoat acrylic paints); Cecilia Determan (my long-lost sibling whose clay creations are what started me on my polymer journey . . . love ya, gal!); Enjoyment Products, Inc., for embossing plates (Glenn Ricci); Kemper Enterprises, Inc., for providing Cernit, Kemper tools, and moral support (Herb Stemphel and Madeline Atilano); Jaquard Products for lending me many beautiful colors of their metallic powders; Rupert Gibbon & Spider, Inc.

Metro Detroit Polymer Art Guild for the world's finest group of polymer artists and for being my bestest buddies!; Milmar, Inc. (Milt Immerman), for allowing me the time to play, experiment, and create, and for believing in my abilities); National Polymer Clay Guild for the focus, information, and inspiration you give me; Polyform Corp. for Sculpey III, PROMAT, Sculpey, Polyform, Super Sculpey, and the best most supportive friends anyone could have (Chuck Steinmann, Wayne Marsh, Hope Phillips, and Donna Kato); Wee Folk, Inc., for the gift you give the world and the support and friendship you give me (Dan and Maureen Carlson); and the Society of Craft Designers for the scholarship that gave my polymer sculptures credibility and for giving me credit for my talent.

Margaret Briggs for her Internet Inkpen design, her knowledge of the "web," and her friendly contributions in Cyberspace to the polymer art world. Margaret is also the editor of the polymer clay home page on the Internet. You can reach her at CBXM13B@prodigy.com; the internet address is http://www.hic.net/polyhome.html.

INTRODUCTION

"What confusion! How *does* a person *choose*? There are so many different clays out there! How do I know which one is right for my project? What's the difference between PROMAT, FIMO, and Cernit? Why do artists prefer certain clays over others? What's the best way or place to obtain large amounts of polymer clay? Where do I get those cute little tools? Where can I take classes? What are the answers, and who do I ask? There are how-to books out there, but they don't give me the answers to these nuts-and-bolts questions! Why is all of this kept such big secret?"

Throughout my career as a polymer artist and product demonstrator, I have been asked these questions and so many more. It's frustrating, to say the least, when there seems to be nobody who knows the answers, and no books to tell you. While each package tells you how to bake (how long for which thickness, what temperature, and so on), nowhere on that package does it say "this product is easier to put through the Klay Gun" or "this product is stronger for wearable art than that product." But, if you are a budding polymer artist, who do you go to? Where's the hotline? Auntie Maude knows about making bread dough sculpture, and the lady down the street uses oil paints, and there are plenty of informational books on sculpture and painting at the book store, but nobody knows or works with polymer clay in your circle of acquaintances. You may well be the first and only "kid" on your block to ever work with polymer clay.

Until recently, when people saw beads and little figurines made of polymer clay, they thought those beads were hand-painted, or those figurines were colored bread dough. Be comforted, though, the ranks are growing, and you are definitely not alone. "Well, if these ranks are growing, and I'm not alone, where's that information? How do I get it? Why all this secrecy? Why haven't the manufacturers put out lots of information on their products?"

Well, the story is really pretty simple. For all the talk about polymer clay being so hot, it's still in its infancy as an art form. In the late 1980s and early 1990s, before a wonderful book that exposed an underground of very talented polymer artists, these clays with their myriad uses and applications went relatively unknown. Before then, polymer clays were considered kids' modeling clay and a craft item used for making dollhouse or model miniatures. A small but dedicated group of artists were using it to make one-of-a-kind sculptures and dolls. On the home crafts front, little round balls of this clay were dropped in boiling water by local Brownie troops to create simple bead necklaces and refrigerator magnets for Mom.

Then, an explosion of creativity erupted in a niche group brazenly calling themselves "polymer clay artists." These artists constructed incredibly ornate and intricate designs with this clay. What was the catalyst that exposed this boon of creativity throughout the United States?

A pioneering book (now the bible of polymer) called *The New Clay* by Nan Roche appeared on the bookshelves. As soon as the book was cracked open by unsuspecting browsers, they became buyers. The amazing artwork contained within it dazzled the senses. A polymer revolution was thrust upon the U.S. arts and crafts world. Not only was this clay *not* just a kid's modeling clay, but those innocuous little squares of solid color could be transformed into true works of art. Many "readers-turned-artists" then rushed headlong into the pursuit (myself included) of a new artistic life, hungry for related products, different clays, information, and classes on this incredible "new" substance.

A national guild was formed, hundreds of artists throughout the world joined, and informational and designing inroads through hard hours of trial and tribulation were made. We searched for sources, written, and practical, on this mysterious substance that was not quite a clay and not quite a paint. We formed our own support groups with separate guilds, chapters, and organizations spanning the country. We made major inroads of acceptance in both the craft and the art communities. *The New Clay* was the

catalyst. It focused a group of far-flung unconnected artists, and it began an era of artistic creativity the world hasn't seen since the Renaissance.

As inspiring as the book is (it holds the undisputed distinction of being the original "Owner's Guide to Polymer Clay"), polymer clay was so new that in 1990 when the book was published it could not be everything to everyone. There was much to be learned. Thus, it left an understandable gap in the practical information one needed to determine which clays did what and which ones were best for what you needed.

The New Clay was a gallery meant to shock the senses, to stimulate the possibilities, to awaken the mind and heart of a prolific sleeping giant. This book, as with many others since *The New Clay*, has only been needed to fill the gaps created by the opening of the door. Since then, the growth in the polymer clay industry has enabled myself and others to fill some of those gaps, and to tap into another small part of the infinite range of possibilities of this incredible material.

There could be volumes written on color mixing alone. Reams could be spent on sculpting technique, dollmaking, or jewelry application. This book is different in that it not only focuses on the application of polymer clay to various surfaces to create functional items for home decor but also helps to fill some of the gaps regarding practical information.

As more and more people discover polymer clay, new artists will invent new applications, techniques, and uses for polymer clay. There will be many new support products developed, and the clay will change as needs and times change. Already, there are plans in the works for new formulas, colors, and looks of clays. There are even discussions being held about taking the slight odor out of the polymer clays as they bake. Maybe, as the clays improve, and as polymer artists progress, there will be a company that will take on the challenge of custom-formulating clays to their specific needs! There is a long history (over thirty years!) of polymer development and growth. We are on the threshold of a new era!

Part One

POLYMER CLAY

BASICS

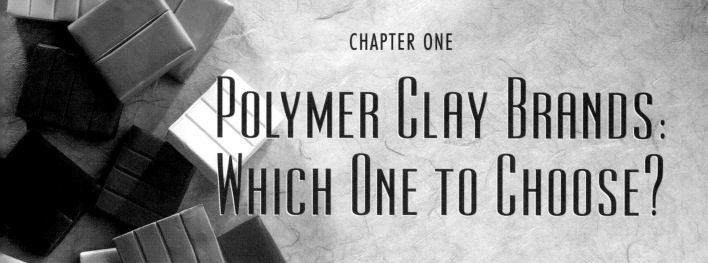

CHAPTER ONE

POLYMER CLAY BRANDS: WHICH ONE TO CHOOSE?

*T*here are many brands of polymer clay on the market. These brands share a number of similarities and differences. Similarities include color range, a polymer base (which means they can be inter-mixed), package amounts (Fig. 1-1), and methods of dividing packages (Fig. 1-2). Differences include such obvious charac-teristics as translucency/opacity, workabili-ty, hardness before and after curing (or baking), and shelf life. There are distinct differences in color saturation and inten-sity, and some brands, such as Granitex, have a textured look. Others resemble metals or pearls or have a glittery look. Some have a flat patina once baked; others cure to a semigloss. Some look like porcelain, some crackle and bubble when baked, and others are milky white and translucent.

The eight most widely available brands of polymer clays are:

Cernit
FIMO
Friendly Clay
Granitex
PROMAT
Sculpey III
Sculpey/Polyform
Super Sculpey

The subsequent chapters will clear up some of the mysteries about polymer clay and give you the information you need to decide intelligently which clays will work best for the things you want to make.

FIG. 1-1 POPULAR POLYMER CLAYS

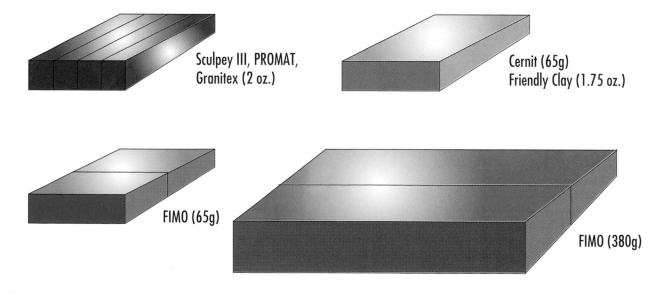

Sculpey III, PROMAT, Granitex (2 oz.)

Cernit (65g)
Friendly Clay (1.75 oz.)

FIMO (65g)

FIMO (380g)

FIG. 1-2 DIVIDING DIFFERENT CLAY BRANDS

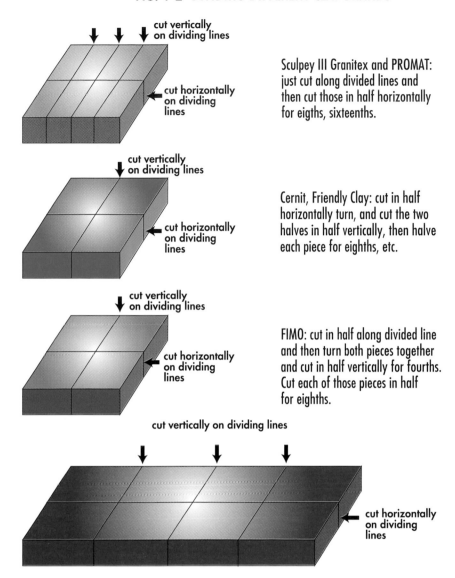

cut vertically on dividing lines

cut horizontally on dividing lines

Sculpey III Granitex and PROMAT: just cut along divided lines and then cut those in half horizontally for eigths, sixteenths.

cut vertically on dividing lines

cut horizontally on dividing lines

Cernit, Friendly Clay: cut in half horizontally turn, and cut the two halves in half vertically, then halve each piece for eighths, etc.

cut vertically on dividing lines

cut horizontally on dividing lines

FIMO: cut in half along divided line and then turn both pieces together and cut in half vertically for fourths. Cut each of those pieces in half for eighths.

cut vertically on dividing lines

cut horizontally on dividing lines

A Survey of the Clays

This chapter clarifies the differences between many of the popular brands of polymer clay and provides a quick-and-easy method for determining which clay will work best for your project. Each brand of polymer clay is discussed and graphs are included at the end of the chapter which outline the following properties of the clays: color intensity (opacity, translucency, texture), workability (conditioning times), tensile strength (durability or toughness), and baking temperatures. To enhance your knowledge and to get you ready for your next project, the chapter also provides a discussion of those qualities that cannot be fully addressed in a graph.

Cernit

Cernit is consistently the most transparent of all the clays, meaning that if it is thin, it will display light through it when held up to a light. Billed as looking the most like porcelain, Cernit No. 1 and opaque white Cernit resemble the "flat" porcelain that has no sheen to its finish, similar to those deli-

CERNIT POLYMER CLAY.

cate Madame Pompadour figurines you see with the Victorian dresses, perfectly coiffed hair, and tiny delicate roses on their fans. It is an "in between" clay in terms of workability. It is soft right from the package, so it takes little time to condition—roll it through the pasta machine a few times or knead it for about five minutes. If you find that the clay is too soft, especially if you have very warm hands, leach the plasticizer out of the clay by placing it between two clean sheets of triple-folded typing paper and weighting it with a heavy book for a day or so until the clay is a bit less oily.

Cernit is probably the stickiest of all the polymer clay brands, so be sure to use a light touch when working with it on warm days. For example, if you are doing bas-relief, you can add pieces of Cernit to the work without pressing hard on those delicate areas, as you must with other, less-sticky clays.

Because of its superior tensile strength, Cernit is an ideal choice for building durable wearable art, such as buttons, pins, and earrings. It is also the easiest clay to polish or buff to a dazzling shine and can look for the world like glass. It is available in 65-gram (2.25-ounce) packages.

Even though Cernit's colors have a transparent base, the company manufactures an opaque white, so that you can make your colors brighter and denser, similar in appearance to FIMO. With FIMO, you need a large amount of translucent and a small amount of color to make it translucent. With Cernit, you need about one-third opaque white to two-thirds color to make it opaque. Hence, faux or imitative techniques are as easily achieved with Cernit as they are with FIMO—you just need to follow slightly different rules.

Cernit is extremely strong and pliable when baked at near-maximum temperatures for a long period of time and left in the oven to cool. I've demonstrated Cernit's pliability at trade shows by forming a piece of the clay into a thin, half-moon about

$1/16$ inch thick and inviting people to bend it and flex it. (I even wrote on it in indelible ink, "Bend me, flex me, I'm Cernit.") This convinced many people of its strength and durability, and only after two trade shows of constant torture by many hands, did the clay begin to tear—not crack—at its major stress point.

Many artists choose Cernit for items that will be handled a lot, such as buttons and wearables (for example, necklaces, earrings, bangle bracelets), and for one-of-a-kind dolls. Its highly translucent quality and realistic skin tones make it a great choice for dollmakers around the world.

FIMO

FIMO polymer clay is made by Eberhard Faber in Neumarkt, Germany. It comes in forty-two gorgeous colors; six "stone colors," similar in appearance to Polyform's Granitex; "glamour" (subtly glittered) colors; and two formulas of translucent. One of the translucent formulas, art translucent (00), only comes in 380-gram, or 13-ounce, packages. What distinguishes it from other translucent formulas is that it cracks and bubbles just beneath the surface as it bakes, an effect that artists doing faux effects or imitative techniques prefer. The other transparent (01) is not really transparent; it is FIMO's noncracking formula of translucent clay. FIMO is available in 65-gram (2.25-ounce) packages. All colors including stone colors are also available in the larger economy size, the 380-gram (13-ounce) package.

Polymer clay aficionados love FIMO's quality, finished durability, firm consistency, and richly opaque colors. You can adjust the opaqueness of FIMO, make it more translucent, by adding various amounts of art translucent (00) or transparent (01) FIMO. For the millefiori technique, an artist usually prefers the stark contrast offered by the opaque clays. The reduction of the cane's design is more obvious; a tiny design is easier to see if there is higher contrast

FIMO POLYMER CLAY.

(color and opacity) in the clay. Artists using faux or imitative techniques, such as those to recreate semiprecious stones like jade and amber, prefer to use smaller amounts of opaque clay and larger amounts of translucent clay.

Artists who work with FIMO are convinced of its superior qualities: It has negligible differences in color and dye lots, the quality control is excellent, and it is a "serious" artists' medium, the Rolls Royce of polymer clays. The nature of FIMO is that its firmness increases with time within certain limits. As some colors of FIMO are sold faster than other colors, it can happen that the firmness of FIMO varies from color to color. Therefore, conditioning time varies from color to color.

Continuing from batch-to-batch, year-after-year, this inconsistency can produce mixed results in your finished work, especially if you are new to the clay, do not know what these inconsistencies may lead to, or do not know how to deal effectively with them. Experienced FIMO artists have learned to make note of these inconsistencies and adjust. Because most of the projects in this book involve applying mixed color to a surface, rather than moving or shifting softer colors as in the millefiori technique, this inconsistency will be negligible.

According to Eberhard Faber, manufacturer of FIMO, under proper conditions, FIMO is usable up to ten years or more. Storage temperatures should not exceed 40 degrees Celsius to 104 degrees Celsius. However, once it is exposed to heat for a period of time, it becomes difficult to work with straight from the package; in effect, it becomes partially cured. To keep your newly purchased clays from hardening prematurely, see "Storing Your Polymer Clay" on page 35.

Eberhard Faber has devised a unique internal production code system for following up on the quality of each package of FIMO. This code appears on each package below and to the left of the color name. It usually begins with a letter followed by a number, such as B 6, C 4, D 5, and so on.

If you end up with a package of hard, ten-year-old clay, you can fix the problem with determination, a firm hand, additives, and a food processor. If you have a hand or wrist condition (for example, carpal tunnel syndrome, weak wrists, or weak hand muscles), this clay can be a challenge, if not a possible danger, so listen to your body, do only what feels right, and follow the conditioning instructions below.

Conditioning FIMO

If the FIMO in the store is hard, don't buy it. FIMO becomes ever softer with each fresh shipment, so if you purchased a semi-baked package of clay, return it, and ask for fresher clay. If you have older clay sitting at home and you cannot return it, take the trauma out of conditioning it by hand by using one or more of the following: Mix Quick, mineral oil, a food processor, a pasta machine, a heating pad, and/or water and a tightly sealed plastic bag.

Mix Quick Conditioning

Purchase Mix Quick Kneading Medium to soften clay and make it easier to condition. If you use it sparingly (1/4 ounce Mix Quick to one ounce FIMO), Mix Quick will not alter the clay's color or consistency noticeably.

Oil Conditioning

Use one drop of baby oil or mineral oil or two drops of hand lotion that contains mineral oil per two-ounce block of FIMO to condition stubborn clay. Chop the FIMO into small pieces (about one-inch squares) before dropping them into the food processor. Mix until the squares begin to clump together like large curd cottage cheese. If the clay begins to stick to the bottom of the processor, stop the motor, scrape the clay out with a metal spatula, and drop the clay piece-by-

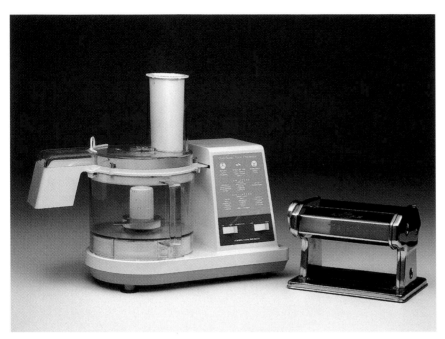

Food processor (left) used to condition clay and a hand crank pasta machine (right) used to condition clay and then roll it into long, thin sheets.

piece back into the processor. The clay should begin to lump together, similar to bread dough when it is mixed, and a large ball of clay may form and twirl around inside the bowl. *Don't allow this ball to become too large or to twirl too long; you can damage the motor by mixing the clay too long.* When you remove the clay from the bowl, it should be warm, sticky, pliable, and elastic. You can then roll the clay into snakes for immediate use, or you can run it though a pasta machine until the clay is glossy, smooth, and even in color.

Food Processor

A food processor is essential for preparing and conditioning large amounts of FIMO. It can be a life (hand) saver if your clay is stiff or hard. I prefer the Hamilton Beach dual speed, because it is sturdy, relatively quiet compared with the other brands, and moderately priced, but feel free to try any well-constructed brand. Simply make sure that the metal blades attach to the bottom of the blade-column assembly and that the machine has a large enough motor so it will

dice even the driest and hardest clays and will not be overtaxed when you conditioning large amounts of clay for extended periods.

Practice safety to avoid injury. *Never reach into the bowl while the blade is moving.* (Most newer food processors have a safety feature that prevents the blades from turning when the lid is off.) *Do not use the bowl or blades for anything other than polymer clay.* If you cannot afford another processor for your food, purchase another bowl and blades and keep it in the kitchen. (Most manufacturers include a toll-free number with warranty and product information, so if you have difficulty finding parts in a retail store, you can purchase them through mail-order. With proper care and maintenance, the machine will last through many years of clay processing.)

After continually using the food processor to condition your clay, you may notice a permanent polymer glaze embedded in the plastic of the bowl. This is due to those insidious plasticizers eating into the bowl's plastic finish. However, your bowl won't disintegrate; it will just look a little dirty or cloudy. You can remedy some of the problem by cleaning the bowl after each round of conditioning with isopropyl alcohol and an old clean terry-cloth rag. I clean the bowl with the rag to remove any remaining clay between rounds; then when I have finished conditioning the rest of the colors, I clean it with the alcohol to remove any polymer residue.

Condition only what you need in shifts of 4 to 5 ounces per shift in the larger food processors, 2 to 3 ounces in the Black and Decker Handy Choppers, or smaller food processors. If you are conditioning large amounts of clay in many colors, condition the lightest colors first, followed by successively darker and darker colors. Dump the conditioned clay out onto a clean work surface: Glass, Plexiglas, Lexan, or secured white paper will work well. Knead small clumps that are comfortable to hold in the palm of your hand. Condition by rolling the congealed lump in a back-and-forth motion between your two palms; then repeat the process. If you are disabled in one hand, roll the clay into a snake on the work surface, fold in half, and roll again.

The FIMO is fully conditioned when it is pliable, rubbery, soft, and shiny. When you pick it up, it should stretch freely, without "snapping" apart easily. It should look totally blended in color, with no streaks, crumbling edges, inconsistencies, or hard lumps. In short, it should feel like warm putty in your hands.

Pasta Machine

Use a pasta machine to help you condition FIMO. This method takes a bit more time and is often combined with the food processor method to condition and even out the texture of the clay. However, never try to run unconditioned FIMO through a pasta machine; always work the clay first. Knead the FIMO into a flattened slab. Place the slab between the two rollers, adjust the thickness setting to the widest (usually setting one), and turn the crank clockwise to draw the clay through the blades (Fig. 1-3). (If you turn the crank counterclockwise, it will eject the clay.) If the clay crumbles, pick the pieces up, press them together, flatten them out

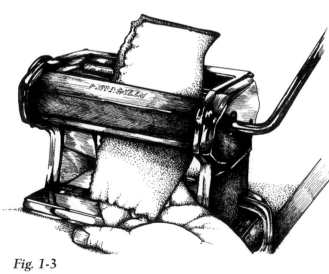

Fig. 1-3

tortilla-style, and feed the clay "tortilla" through the pasta machine again. Repeat this process, turning and folding the clay in half, placing the fold-side into the blades first to let the air-bubbles out, until there are no crumbles.

The FIMO is fully conditioned when it is shiny, rubbery, ultra-smooth, and glossy and the edges are relatively smooth and sharp, not crumbly. Between each run through the machine, you may wish to tighten the setting a notch: Simply fold the clay in half, run it through a few times, turning and folding as you go, then run it through the next tighter setting. You can roll FIMO fairly thin, although setting seven is maximum for any practical purposes; I generally stop at setting four. At too thin a setting, the clay will adhere to the roller when it makes the full revolution and stick to the blades and underworkings, or the cleaning plate (the area beneath the first roller where the excess clay accumulates). If you start seeing "other color" streaks or particles in your clay, check the cleaning plate, and follow the suggestions for cleaning it under "Cleaning Your Pasta Machine" on page 34.

As with any art material, safety and good maintenance habits are paramount. With proper care and cleaning, your pasta machine will be an indispensable tool for years to come.

Heating Pad

The heating pad is another useful tool for conditioning FIMO. I recommend using an old heating pad (one you won't be using for your body anymore) and dedicating it to warming your clay. Slide the pad under your work surface,

GRANITEX POLYMER CLAY.

place the clay on top, and leave it there until it is warm to the touch, about five minutes. When it's finished, you'll be left with soft clay that's easy to work. Remember not to set the heating pad on high or to leave the clay heating for too long. I have accidentally prebaked my clay by doing just that. In this case, I left it warming for a half hour and came back to discover that the first quarter-inch of the diameter of the clay was solidly baked and the inside warm and toasty. (This was a rather expensive mistake because it was a 13-ounce package.)

When working with FIMO, don't work more clay than you can comfortably fit in your hand, relax with it, and work it slowly. Make friends with it. Take the time to actually feel the clay become softer and more pliable.

Warm Water and Bag

The warm water and bag method is another way to condition a hard block of FIMO. Check to make sure that the bag you are using does not leak; otherwise, you will have a temporary mess on your hands. A thick, 6-milliliter plastic zip-closure bag works wonderfully. Immerse the clay in water that is slightly warmer than body, or around 100 degrees. Allow the clay to sit undisturbed for ten to fifteen minutes, remove the bag, dry it, and work the clay into condition by kneading it, rolling it back and forth between your palms, and repeating the process until the clay is fully conditioned.

Heat Conditioning

Heat conditioning is the least expensive, most direct method of conditioning small amounts of FIMO. If you are not going to be a frequent user of the clay, this is the best method for you. Set the clay under an incandescent light for awhile to warm it, then cut the block of FIMO into small, thin slices. Condition it slowly and carefully by kneading it in your hands and rolling the

slices between your two palms or on the work surface.

FIMO's Stone Colors

In response to the ever-changing and growing line of American polymer clays, FIMO's maker, Eberhard Faber, introduced stone colors in Fall 1995. These six colors, China jade, granite, jasper, lapis lazuli, rose quartz, and turquoise, are similar in appearance to those in Polyform's Granitex line; however, there are subtle differences. Granite, or the blackish gray-colored clay with a translucent base, has flat round black granules and small metallic or silver sparkles embedded in it. Lapis lazuli is the only other stone color to have these sparkles. While the clay is softer than regular FIMO (although not as soft as Granitex), it still holds its characteristic shape and has FIMO's tensile strength. The manufacturer's baking temperature is 265 degrees.

FRIENDLY CLAY

Friendly Clay is another polymer clay available to artists. Manufactured in Taiwan and imported by the American Art Clay Company, this clay spans the gap between FIMO and Sculpey III: It is less expensive than FIMO, available in smaller-sized packages than Sculpey III (1.75 ounces), and aimed at a more general craft store audience, making it great for students. It comes in twenty-four colors, including transparent, two pearlized colors, light pink, and light blue. The clay can be quite difficult to condition, even harder than FIMO at times; however, Friendly Clay is malleable if you purchase a package that is newer, has not been on the store shelf for a long time, and has not been exposed to heat, sunlight, or ultraviolet light for a prolonged period of time.

Friendly Clay is more similar to FIMO in workability than any other polymer clay. It even looks like FIMO when it is cured and has similar colors. The manufacturer's baking time is twenty to thirty minutes at 265

PROMAT AND SCULPEY III POLYMER CLAYS.

degrees, although I tend to bake it at a lower temperature, 250 to 260 degrees, and leave it in longer. I cool all of my pieces in the oven, regardless of brand, to make them stronger and more resilient.

Friendly Clay's tensile strength is comparable to FIMO's. If baked properly, it is resilient to breakage. It has all of the same abilities as other polymer clays and is intermixable and compatible with other brands. If you need to soften Friendly Clay use any of the methods described under Conditioning FIMO, or Friendly Clay softener or Mix Quick Kneading Medium; however, the Friendly Clay softener is less expensive and was formulated to be used with the clay.

The same storage and clean-up rules that apply to all the other clays also apply to Friendly Clay.

GRANITEX

Polyform's newest addition, Granitex is billed as the polymer clay you can "Take for Granite." It is a catchy slogan, but as with black Granitex, it accurately imitates the stone. Granitex is available in 2-ounce packages, in eight pastel colors.

Granitex feels and works similarly to Sculpey III, because the base mixtures are the same. It it is, however, a bit drier than Sculpey III, perhaps because of the small baked particles, or "fibers," suspended within the clay itself. It bakes to about the same tensile strength as Sculpey III and becomes brittle when it is either baked too thin or not baked on a support surface of metal, glass, papier mâché, wood, or aluminum foil. When baked in a solid-core sphere (bead shape) without projectiles, it is durable and strong. If you are baking the clay on a support surface, I recommend baking about twenty to thirty percent longer and 5 degrees lower than what is recommended on the package and then cooling the clay in the oven. (You may also want to use this method when using Sculpey III.)

Granitex can be used in place of Sculpey III because the clays are identical, barring any differences in color and texture. You can also use Granitex for canework, but I recommend outlining each Granitex color in a solid Sculpey III color for the high contrast you will need for the cane to have definition in the design. This clay is ripe with possibilities, and as the polymer community discovers it, it will be used in more innovative ways.

PROMAT

Many serious artists use PROMAT, one of the finest American-made polymer clays. Available in 2-ounce packages, this clay recently underwent some interesting and much needed changes: It became more opaque, richer in color, stronger, and more flexible and several new colors were introduced, bringing its color line to thirty.

PROMAT is the only brand to have *colored* glow-in-the-dark clay; it comes in such colors as orange, green, and pink and is called Nightglow. PROMAT is the most brilliantly pearlescent of all the polymers—its red, blue, and green festive, Christmas bulb-like metallics, its silver, gold, and copper the most realistically metallic. It has eight new "designer" colors, two of which are in response to FIMO's discontinuation of the sadly missed olive green and brick red colors. It has an imitation of FIMO's anthracite called graphite as well as translucent and white pearl (these last two are comparable to their competitors, but the colors already exist in Sculpey III.)

PROMAT's new formulation may be a slight adjustment for some, but it is well worth it for the improvements. It looks and feels less waxy, has more defined and brighter color, holds its shape exceedingly well, and is quite resistant to fingerprints. On the tensile-strength scale, I rate it a nine, with Cernit as its nearest competitor, slightly stronger at a ten.

Occasionally, you may encounter an

older batch of PROMAT that has become hard and requires additional conditioning. You can use a softening agent called Solid Diluent, which is available from Polyform (see Resources on page 89). Just add a tiny pinch of it to the PROMAT and mix it in by hand, or soften the clay in the food processor (see page 8). Solid Diluent can be used to soften any of the Polyform clays, although it is rarely needed for the others, because they are already quite soft. You may also use Super Elasticlay to soften hard, out-of-the-package PROMAT. Again, add just about ⅛ to ¼ ounce of Super Elasticlay to a 2-ounce package of PRO-MAT. It will not only soften and condition the clay, but it will help make it more flexible, making the clay even stronger.

SCULPEY III

Sculpey III is one product in a group of American-made polymer clays. Its partners are PROMAT, Granitex, Sculpey/Polyform, and Super Sculpey, all manufactured by Polyform, Inc. The Polyform clays are similar in terms of general workability and have a drier feel than their German-made competitors, FIMO and Cernit. However, they are quite different from one another in their tensile strength, color range, workability, and appearance.

Sculpey III is the most colorful of the Polyform clays. Its range includes forty colors. The colors are organized under categories that describe what you should expect when you use them: "Brights," "Intermediates," "Basics," and "Pearls." Each category contains ten colors.

The Pearls contain soft pastels: light blue, pink, and pearl (white). These subtly glittered shades are reminiscent of satin or dyed pearls. There are also stronger, bolder tones that mimic precious metals and alloys, such as copper, gold, and silver. There are "surprises" in the Pearl shades, too: The blue is rich and vibrant, the green woodsy and dark, the lilac soft and rich.

The Brights and Basics are more similar in appearance, but their intensities are quite different when compared side-by-side. The Brights are brighter, as their name suggests, and can be quite shocking in appearance. Basic red is an almost-ripe tomato color, Basic green a brilliant "kelly," and there are eight more colors. Then there are the "neon Bright" colors: Hot Pink, Lime, Atomic Orange, and Red Hot Red. Rounding out the Brights are ivory, turquoise, purple, violet, mint, and lemon. Also among the Basics is translucent, a noncolor favored by artists for faux or imitative techniques, such as those used to recreate semiprecious stones like jade, coral, amber, lapis, and pearl.

The Intermediates are the newest additions in the Sculpey III line and are the most opaque, with a white base added to give the colors that Intermediate tone. Each color is categorically unique: Intermediate Dusty Rose is an intense raspberry shake color, Lavender truly lavender, and Leaf Green a half-and-half mix between olive and spring green. There is a true navy blue, a lovely terra-cotta, a leather-like tan, a rich teal as well as a maroon and a coral. What's more, these clays are constantly evolving, and as they do new colors may be added to the line.

What to Expect from Sculpey III

Sculpey III is renowned for its softness and workability. Available in 2-ounce packages, Sculpey III is more easily conditioned directly from the package. If you have a hand condition like carpal tunnel syndrome or if you are a beginner, a child, or a production-conscious artist without much clay-conditioning time, you will love Sculpey III for its overall softness.

Unlike FIMO, which has colors that are predictably softer than others (notably black and white), Sculpey III is most predictable when it comes to consistency in workability between colors. Sculpey III's colors are all the same consistency, so your canework is more evenly reduced. This consistency is important because it affects the outcome of certain projects. For example, if the colors have differing softnesses and you are using the millefiori technique, the colors will tend to "move" at different rates within the cane, shifting more if the color is softer. While some artists have found ways to circumvent this problem, by capping, pounding, reducing slowly, and the like, there is less shifting with clays that have that consistency in workability, thus making the outcome of your project more predictable.

Conditioning Sculpey III

There is no trick to conditioning Sculpey III. Unlike FIMO, Cernit, Friendly Clay, and PROMAT, Sculpey III requires minimal conditioning before you begin the actual project. Straight from the package, the clay is soft and buttery and has the consistency of soft, dry bread dough—that is, barring any cold temperatures inside your home (under 50 degrees in winter). The clay takes about five minutes to condition on a cool day and less on a warm day. If you have a hand-cranked pasta machine (more on this later), you will need to run the clay through six to eight times to condition it. If you don't have one, knead, roll, and squeeze the clay until it is warm and pliable, about five minutes.

Sculpey III Baking Time and Temperature

The manufacturer recommends baking Sculpey III for fifteen minutes per ¼ inch of thickness at 275 degrees.

> **WARNING:** *Never* microwave Sculpey III or any other polymer clay, because doing so will cause the clay to heat at different temperatures. As a result, the clay will bubble, crack, burn, and *if it reaches an overall temperature above 290 degrees, it will release a noxious fume.* Therefore, read all manufacturer's directions before baking, buy and use a separate oven thermometer every time you bake, and remember that baking any brand of polymer clay can be hazardous to your health if you burn it, so bake with caution.

SCULPEY/POLYFORM

According to Charles (Chuck) Steinmann, president of Polyform, polyform clay had a humble start. It was used as electrical insulation in hot boxes, where it could absorb the heat generated by the electrical current. (The heat formed a strong, solid, insulating bond in the polyform between the critical parts.) It provided a safe alternative to other degenerative types of insulation and was less expensive, but the market was limited. Then someone (and I don't know exactly who) realized that this low-bake, relatively strong material had potential in the arts and crafts market. It was perfect: It cured at a low temperature, needed no special or expensive tools, such as kilns and throwing wheels, and needed no glazes, paints, or fired finishes.

With that in mind, the company decided that *Polyform* was not descriptive enough for the arts and crafts market in the early 1960s, so it coined the name *Sculpey*. Since that time, sculptors, artisans, crafters, moldmakers, and miniaturists have grown the clay from plain white glop into a multicolored "intermixable" modeling compound.

Although Sculpey has been replaced by succeeding generations of polymer clays, all under the Polyform label, there are two products that are still uncolored and closer in formulation to the original product than the colored clays: Polyform and Sculpey. These two products are identical, but some users would argue that there are distinct differences. Sculpey III, PROMAT, and Granitex are their successors, yet all of the Polyform clays generally contain the same basic ingredients, just in differing amounts and colors.

Polyform and Sculpey are terrific for kids and for finished items that will be sitting on a shelf undisturbed. They are less expensive than other clays and they come in wonderful bulk sizes for the classroom and large-scale sculptor. They are easy to handle, moldable, and have all the qualities of Sculpey III. Although the clays only come in white, you can do marvelous things with them. If you like to paint, airbrush, or shade and float colors onto surfaces, these clays are ideal. You can also use them to make jewelry. I recommend round beads or beads without any added projectiles, because these clays tend to be more fragile than the rest.

SUPER SCULPEY

Super Sculpey is Polyform's dollmaking clay and is used by many of the country's foremost one-of-a-kind dollmakers. Super Sculpey comes only in a pinkish tan color. It is somewhere between PROMAT and Sculpey III in tensile strength, meaning that it is not as flexible as PROMAT and not as brittle as Sculpey III. Some artists use it straight from the package and others mix it with varying amounts of Cernit and FIMO. Many dollmakers experiment with mixing their own formulas, keeping the exact ratios a secret. The outcome usually involves per-

sonal preference in color, opacity, finished look, strength, workability, and doll style.

Super Sculpey can be temperamental. Baking the clay at too high a temperature can discolor and darken the clay, creating uneven area blotches, small white crescent-shaped bubbles, or irregularities just beneath the clay's surface. However, many of these bubbles can be traced to improper conditioning. To condition Super Sculpey and help eliminate some of those bubbles, knead it, roll it though the pasta machine, slap it on the work surface several times, and, if preferred, wedge the clay for ten minutes or more before sculpting. (Wedging is the method organic clay artists use to "bang" the bubbles out of the clay before sculpting or throwing.)

Super Sculpey accepts tooling, drilling, sanding, and polishing as well as any polymer clay and is used in everything from large-scale models to tiny miniatures with great results.

CHART 1 POLYMER CLAY TENSILE STRENGTH

(TEN being strongest and most flexible, ONE being most brittle)

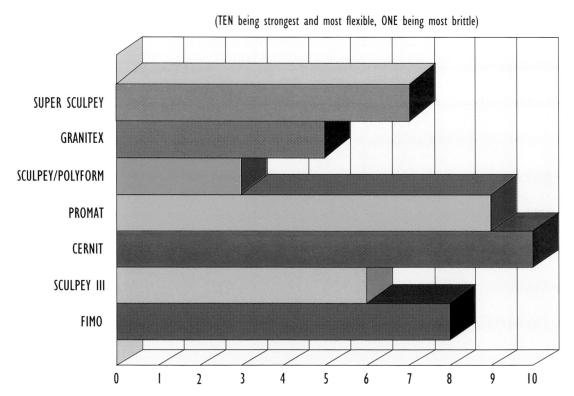

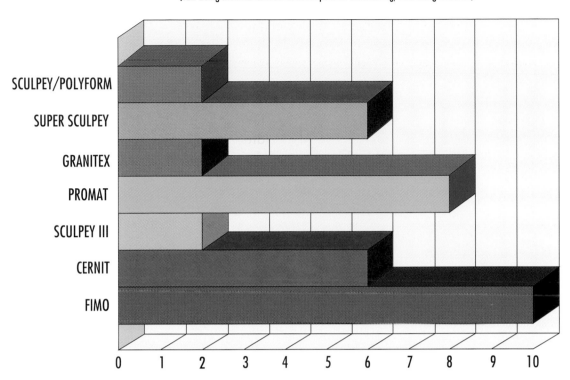

CHART 2 POLYMER CLAY CONDITIONING TIME SCALE
(TEN being the most amount of time spent on conditioning, ONE being the least)

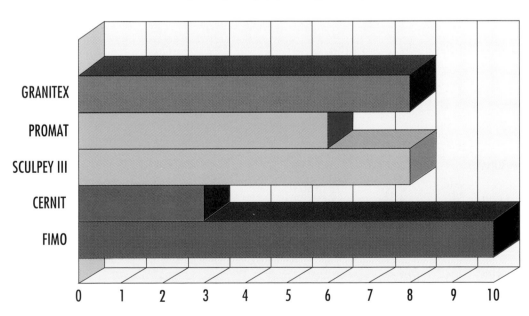

CHART 3 POLYMER CLAY COLOR INTENSITY SCALE
(TEN being most opaque, ONE being most transparent)

WORKING WITH THE CLAYS

GENERAL WORK SURFACE GUIDELINES

Your work surface should be clean, dry, smooth, and made from a material that will not stain from the polymer clay. The clay is insidiously destructive to wood and wood finishes, because it seeps into the fiber, stains it, and eventually breaks down the wood's varnish or finish. Wood is not a good work surface because it is grainy and has a slightly uneven texture that the clay will pick up every time it passes over the surface. I prefer a large sheet of tempered glass for three reasons: (1) It does not scratch or warp, (2) it cleans up well, and (3) you can bake your project on it as long as it fits into your oven.

Tempered glass is ideal for large or numerous pieces and can be used over and over again, because it is strong and thick. You can make the glass easier to grip when retrieving it from the oven by taping one edge with masking tape. If you allow your polymer pieces to cool in the oven as I do, you won't need a potholder, only the tape strip. You can purchase tempered glass through a glazier, although you will probably have to order it to your size specifications. It will take some time for the glazier to manufacture it; mine took two weeks. It's an expensive item (a small

8 X 10-inch sheet cost me $18), but with proper care, it will last you a lifetime.

There are less expensive, lightweight alternatives to tempered glass, one of which is clear or milky Lexan. It is quite strong (although it will crack if you bend it too far), and with care it will serve you well and last a long time. Because it is portable and lightweight, it is ideal for the traveling polymer artist. I use several 11 X 17-inch sheets for my students when I am teaching both in my studio and away, to ensure that we will each have a clean, smooth work surface. It is available in small and large sheets at your local hardware store, home center, or department store. The sheets are comparatively inexpensive.

Because Lexan is a highly polished hard plastic, it develops surface scratches easily, scratches that are often then transferred onto your work. Unless it is kept scrupulously clean, it becomes a magnet for clay residue. The solution: Clean Lexan regularly with a good swabbing of isopropyl alcohol and a clean absorbent rag (more on clean-up later).

You can also buy a thick Lucite, which resists scratches but is quite expensive, or a smooth slate or polished marble slab at a kitchen supply store. If you're on a budget, find an old unscratched formica-covered piece of countertop with the wooden or Masonite base still attached. Square it up to the size you will need and make that your work surface. You can also tape a piece of white typing paper to your work area, dispose of it when stained, and replace with a clean sheet of new paper!

Successfully Lighting Your Work Area

Lighting the work area is something most people don't do well, neglect, or think is unimportant. I cannot stress enough the importance of good lighting here. Eye strain is uncomfortable, it inhibits your ability to focus well, and it causes a variety of residual problems, including headaches, tension, fatigue, and muscle tightness in your neck and shoulders. Lighting is also important in placing those details in your project where you want them. One good gooseneck lamp with a 60-watt bulb over your work area can save hours of fatigue and eye strain. Because I wear trifocals (and a heavy prescription for far-sightedness), my glasses magnify the light; the lighter the work surface, the more intense the light, and the easier my eyes fatigue. If your work surface is tempered glass or clear Lexan, place a sheet of pastel paper under it to minimize the brightness if your desktop or counter is white. However, this can create a problem because you can get a false reading on your clay colors. If attaining a particular color is essential, place a sheet of white or black paper next to your work area to examine the color there.

Lighting can drastically affect a clay's appearance. By adjusting or changing the surrounding light, you can give your artwork different looks. A white incandescent bulb will cast a blue light over your work area, a regular incandescent bulb a yellow glow. Cool and warm-tinted fluorescent bulbs create other effects. Natural light is, however, by far the most preferable.

Of course, if you are addicted to poly-

mer clay, you will spend many long nights up working over your desk, without natural light. If you are working in the basement, you may not have a window, let alone one that faces north. Natural light is warm and appealing and has a way of relaxing your senses, especially your eyes. If you can move your work area next to a window, do so. Not only will you have a lovely breeze in the summer, but your work area will be better lit, and your work will no doubt improve.

Good Posture

Many artists tend to ignore the importance of maintaining good posture while they work. Sit straight in your chair, with the small of your back fully supported, and relax the tension in your neck and shoulders. You can avoid having your back, shoulder, neck, arm, or wrist cramp by taking a few simple precautions: Don't hunch over your work area; every now and then, stand up, stretch, walk, rotate your head in slow circles, and press your palms flat onto your work surface to relieve strain; put on relaxing music. Support your wrists while you work with a thin pad, a rolled towel, or a wrist-support glove, to reduce the angle into which you are forcing your wrists to perform those repetitive tasks. Ideally, your wrists should be parallel to your work surface, angled not too far upward with your fingers toward the sky and not too far downward.

To relieve any eye strain you experience, take a break. Change your scenery, lie down with a cool cloth over your eyes and close them for a while, or take a relaxing bath or shower.

Polymer clay is a relaxing, entertaining, and stimulating medium. It will hurt you only if you allow it to. Use special care, common sense, and good judgment. All these will enhance the quality of your life with polymer and the results you achieve.

GENERAL USE TOOLS. Clockwise from bottom center: *Sanford Sharpie Extra Fine Point marker, X-ACTO knife, Kemper Klay Gun and discs, spatula or palette knife, tissue slicing blade (in red clay), FISKARS Paper Edger scissors, four Kemper double-tipped Designer Dot sets (center of photo).*

Tool Time

There are plenty of premade tools designed for use with clay. Tools that were originally intended for organic clays, such as the line of Kemper tools, can easily be used with polymer clay. Kemper has a reputation for producing some of the best-made tools in the country and has been making clay and dollmaking tools for over fifty years. They have pattern cutters in various shapes and sizes that cut and eject polymer clay like magic. These cutters are indispensable in cutting multiples of a shape quickly, easily, and predictably. They work similarly to cookie cutters in that you roll out a thin flat sheet of clay and press the cutter into the clay. The only time you use the little spring-loaded plunger is when the clay gets stuck in the cutter; you can easily eject your clay by depressing the plunger.

Kemper makes several other useful tools for polymer artists. Their needle tool, or pro tool, has a comfortable balance and feel. It is all-steel and virtually indestructible. The needle and handle are one piece, so the tool will not fall apart. Kemper also makes a set of rose cutters (five sizes of round cutters with a flat ejector piece in the handle), a set of leaf cutters (four sizes of paisley-shaped cutters with the same handle as the rose cutters), and other tools compatible with polymer clay. Lately, some retailers have placed these tools alongside the polymer clays and the books on a rack next to it, so that consumers not only know what these tools are used for but where they are. If you do not have an arts and crafts supply store nearby, you can purchase these tools from a number of other sources (see Resources on page 89).

Kemper also manufactures the Klay Gun,

a device that extrudes softened, warmed polymer clay through interchangeable discs, producing nineteen distinct and perfect shapes. These shapes include several sizes of single-hole and multihole discs, a triangle, a square, a half-moon, three tri-lobed and one four-lobed shape, and a clever ribbon-making disc in three sizes. Artists have used them for cane construction, trim pieces, miniature food, animal and human hair, leaves, flowers, ribbon trims on doll dresses, and more.

CUSTOMIZING KEMPER CUTTERS

My friend Sue makes the most wonderful polymer clay characters. At a polymer clay guild meeting, I was drawn to see what new and wonderful creations Sue was wearing and displaying. She pointed out a Christmas brooch she had on. The brooch consisted of a tiny polymer rolling pin next to some freshly rolled "ready-to-bake" gingerbread cookie dough, with three of the tiniest gingerbread men I'd ever seen partially cut out of the dough. I was immediately curious as to where she'd bought the cookie cutters to make the little men. Knowing that she obtained her supplies from many different sources, I expected her to tell me that she found them in some obscure cake-decorating or pastry chef supply store in Germany.

"No," she replied, "you have a zillion of these at home! I've been customizing Kemper cutters for years! I thought you knew!" Immediately, I went home, grabbed the needlenosed pliers, and made gingerbread men cookie cutters in three different sizes. Thanks to Sue, a new world of customizing cutters had opened up. I customized one four-petaled cutter into a fleur-de-lis, which makes a wonderful looking holly leaf. I reshaped cutters that had become out of shape from trying to squeeze them into spaces that were too small, and I straightened out some unwelcome kinks.

It's always best to experiment like this with old cutters, and if you buy them in single packages, you'll only be out a couple of

dollars if you obliterate one. Just take your time, squeeze gently with the pliers, avoid using force, or you'll end up breaking the cutter or bending it too far to recover it.

NONTRADITIONAL TOOLS

The fun part of working with polymer clay is using nontraditional tools. Artists like Tory Hughes and Maureen Carlson have invented their own tools and use a variety of found objects to achieve their results. Such objects include nails, screws, household drills, toothpicks, dental tools, pastry tools, cookie cutters, pasta machines, brayers, clay rollers, marble rolling pins, cheese graters, noodle cutters, egg slicers, garlic presses, scissors, pinking shears, FISKARS Paper Edgers, bamboo skewers, styluses, toothbrushes, spatulas, utility knives, wallpaper, single-edged blades, tissue blades, among other things.

Later in the book, I use some of these objects to complete the projects and to help you better see how tools really help make the piece; I also provide a list of Resources in the back of the book (see page 89) to help you find them. There are also a number of instructional books available that tell you where to obtain the manufactured tools, how to make your own, and how to use them.

While many of us primarily use our tools to work the clay in its unbaked or conditioned "raw" state, you can use certain tools to achieve certain results after you bake the clay. How do you get that glossy shine without applying a glaze? What sort of drill do you use to get those perfect holes? Sandpaper, electric buffers, small handheld drills, and interchangeable power tools help you make those finishing touches.

Wet and dry sandpaper in 400, 600, and 1,000 grit is useful for removing fingerprints, imperfections, and bubbles in the clay, while the finest grit paper (the higher the number, the finer the grit) is perfect for polishing the baked polymer to a semigloss.

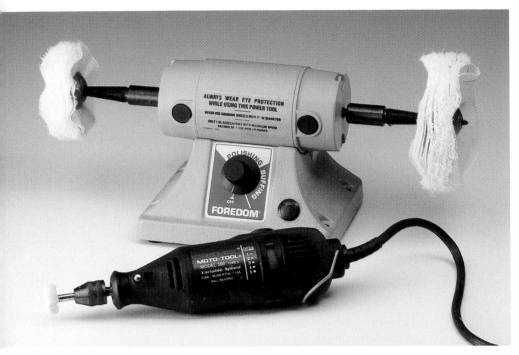

POWER TOOLS. *A Foredom polisher/buffer and a Dremel Mototool for drilling.*

To achieve a high gloss, wet-sand using the largest grit sandpaper (underwater is best, so you will not breathe in the polymer dust), continue wet-sanding with the next higher grit, finish with a soft, clean dry cloth, and buff with a buffing wheel. The polymer will shine like a new car.

POWER TOOLS

If you are production buffing, polishing, or drilling a lot of perfect little holes, you may wish to purchase a handheld Dremel Mototool with a few small muslin buffs and a drill the size you want your finished holes to be. For buffing and polishing larger pieces, a stationary Foredom polisher/buffer or a bench grinder fitted with a soft white muslin buffing wheel works well (Fig. 2-1). When these muslin buffs are new, they shed little threads. To help prevent the small airborne polymer particles from getting into your nose and face, wear a dust mask, and work with the buffer inside a large, stationary cardboard box with the front flaps cut out. Also, follow the safety procedures that came with your power tool to protect yourself from injury.

Safety Tips

When using any power tool, wear safety glasses or goggles to protect your eyes. No matter how securely your are holding the object you are drilling or buffing, kickback or flying objects can injure your eyes if you leave them unprotected. Secure your object in a vise-like tool or, if you must hold the object in your hands, be sure you work inside a cardboard box or under a plastic see-through shield. Buff holding your object at the bottom of the buffing pad, so that the tool doesn't "catch" the item and throw it.

When drilling holes in thick objects, mark where you want the hole with an indelible marker. Use the tip of an X-ACTO or utility knife to drill a pilot hole in which to press the tip of the drill. Hold the object securely on a disposable surface that can be drilled into, such as a block of wood. Drill halfway through the object, turn the object, mark the other side, and drill another pilot hole; then follow the same drilling procedure. *Never* drill the object while you are holding it in the air or toward your hand, lap, or face; the injury can be painful, debilitating, and disfiguring.

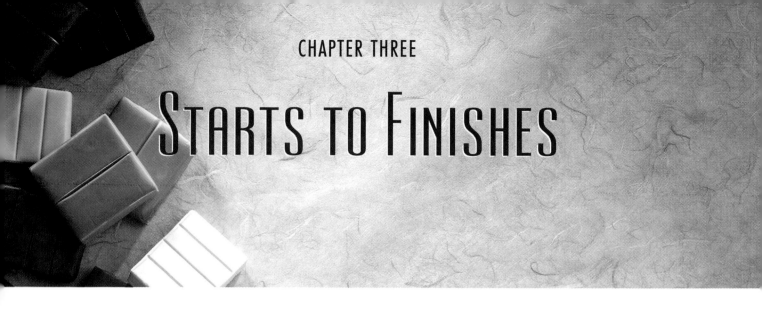

STARTS TO FINISHES

ADDING TEXTURES, COLORS, AND SHAPES

TEXTURES

Textures surround us. Our lives are intertwined with them. The sense of touch is so important that even when we are infants, we must be close to a warm soft and nurturing body to feel safe, secure, and calm. It's one of our first needs.

Artists are drawn not only to see art, but to touch it and experience it—to follow the lines of the sculpture, to feel the coolness of the metal, to run our fingertips lightly over the oil paints lumped onto the Van Gogh canvas (and to set off every alarm in the gallery!). My polymer art has evolved into a much more textural, touchable form, because I do not want it to sit on shelves and gather dust. I want people to be excited about being able to touch my creations. I want them to be functional and satisfying, both visually and tactilely. Polymer clay is so incredible for texture! It can feel cool and dry, yet warm and sensuous. It is truly a feast for the "gotta touch its" in all of us.

Items for Creating Texture

Items for creating texture in your work are equally as important as the right tools. In fact, textures are so easy to use with polymer clay that you can often find them in everyday items. I myself have broken a headlight from my husband's old van and used the inside for a particular texture I wanted to achieve. I've used a strip of lawn chair webbing for the little coat on the old man sculpture, and I've borrowed nails, saws, sandpaper, and other things from my husband's tool collection.

Objects that are junk to most can often create that perfect texture. Tory Hughes is no doubt the most inventive polymer artist I have ever seen when it comes to utilizing textures from cast-off sources. The spools from adding machine tape become a texture for mokume gane, and pencil points and erasers are pressed into the layers. Burlap, leaves, twigs, dirt, sandpaper, sand, and bark are also in her repertoire of found objects.

There are also more controlled texturing tools that produce the same results over and over again. These tools are constructed from material that will not break down over time. They include: heavy material, plastic, plastic canvas, leather, leather-working tools, rubber stamps, and embossing plates. The material, the plastic canvas, and the embossing plates may be carefully rolled into the surface of a rolled piece of clay using a pasta machine. The thicker items, on the other hand, must be pressed into the clay, or the clay must be pressed onto them.

There are no general tips on using texture tools successfully. How you use them

COOKIE CUTTERS AND CLAY CUTTING TOOLS. Left to right, back row: *Kemper leaf and rose cutters, round biscuit cutter set, Kemper pattern cutters.* Middle row: *Plastic Wilton heart-shaped cookie cutter set, Friendly cutters, canapé cutters, small cookie cutters.* Front row: *Kemper pattern cutters, Friendly cutters, Kemper leaf and rose cutters, canapé cutters.*

in your work is entirely up to you and is really self-explanatory. Remember though, polymer clay is an oil-based clay, meaning that any dirt, residue, color, or hair that is on or in the texture tool you are using will end up a permanent memento in your clay, so clean or dust it before using it.

Found Objects

Old, nubby, or dense material, such as burlap (try coating the material first with polyurethane varnish to keep it from shedding), denim, brocade, and lace, has some of the best textures. For the polymer clay not to pick up the bits of fuzz that you embed in it along with these materials, you must wash or literally beat the cloth into a non-fuzzy state before adding it to the clay. Your results can be quite spectacular, especially when you add powder or makeup to a clay surface that you are texturing with heavy lace, before removing the lace.

Nail heads and tips, screws, cookie cutters, store-bought rubber stamps, and leather tools can be pressed into the clay or, in the case of the cookie cutters, can be used to cut shapes from the clay. This works especially well when making Christmas ornaments, magnets, door hangers, gift tags, or faux cookies or candies.

Powders and Potions

Polymer clay picks up and bonds to virtually any substance: It has an oily base that makes it "grab" on to nonoily substances, and it is sticky in its raw state. Artists use these qualities to their advantage with powders (for example, metallic, interference, makeup, and pastels) while the clay is still uncured. You can also use this technique if you don't care for the color of your clay, like the color you get from mixing those ends of canes you don't want to toss in the garbage. Blend the ends into one color and then stroke some makeup or powders over it to make the color a little more interesting.

Artists apply powders in creative and dazzling ways. Sprinkle it onto the surface of the clay to form splotches of color. Lay the clay on paper dusted with powder for a light coating. Mix powder and clay together to create other colors. Add texture to the clay with the powder embedded in it (the clay will just pick up spots of color from

MATERIALS USED FOR CREATING A VARIETY OF FINISHES. Clockwise from top right: *Delta Ceramcoat acrylic paints and Delta waterbase varnish, Eberhard Faber metallic powders, Rub 'n Buff gold one-step finish, and gold composition leafing.*

the texture). Seal the powder into the clay's surface and form a light polymer glaze over it by baking the clay with the powder on it. Because the powder can wear off with vigorous rubbing or dull with constant wear and handling, I recommend applying a polymer clay-compatible coating afterward to seal in the powder.

Potions do not fall easily into any handy or known description. They are a cross between a powder and a paint. The American Art Clay Company's product Rub 'n Buff falls into this category. It is a thick waxy metallic gel, perfect for highlighting an already baked object; a tiny amount on the fingertip is all you need. Rub 'n Buff comes in eighteen shades, with at least six different shades of gold alone.

Dry each potion for the manufacturer's recommended time. Set the finish by baking the piece (regardless of clay brand) for another ten to fifteen minutes at 200 degrees. Seal the finish with a light coating of matte, semigloss, or high-gloss spray lacquer (more on finishes later); brush-on lacquers tend to pull the finish off into the brush or make the finish streaky or dull.

COLORS

Makeup and Paint

Using makeup on polymer clay yields excellent results for color, too. (See "Good Morning, Glory! Garden Soap Dish" on page 66.) Facial powders, blush, eye makeup, and even lipstick powder can be applied to the raw clay first, then baked. Doll artists using polymer clay apply makeup just as makeup artists do: To darken the skin tone, apply a face powder over the entire surface of the clay that is darker than the clay color. To add more lifelike color to the face, apply powdered blush with a soft brush by patting (not stroking it) on. Stroking the blush on in long strokes can cause irreparable streaking, because the clay grabs the

color immediately and absorbs into the clay as it comes off the brush.

Polymer clay quickly absorbs powder colors as well. Because the goal is usually to cover completely the original color of the polymer clay, cover the item with a thick layer of powder, using a heavy hand. Distribute any remaining loose flakes of powder into uncovered or lightly covered areas with a clean brush. For skin tones, use a minimalist approach to create natural looking skin (for example, a light coating of blush on a baby's cheeks will create a more realistic look than a thick coating).

Paints are usually applied after the polymer clay is cured. Polymer artists traditionally use acrylic paints rather than oils, because they are more compatible with the clay. In effect, they dull the patina of the clay and create a "flat" appearance.

I have mixed acrylic paints into raw clay, applied them onto raw clay, and found that doing so does not adversely affect the clay. Because the paints are water based, the paint just makes the clay temporarily mushy. Experiment, apply the paint while the clay is raw, and use your creativity to discover a new technique.

SHAPES

Making and Using Molds

Another wonderful attribute of polymer clay is its versatility. You can make molds from found objects, or you can make an original sculpture yourself, bake it, and then use it as a positive for the mold (see diagrams and/or photos).

Because all of the polymer clays hold such detail, there is no preferred brand for making molds. As long as the mold is thick enough, baked properly for maximum strength, and not overbaked once the polymer is pushed into it, molds made from polymer clays are extremely durable and work well. There are several types of poly-

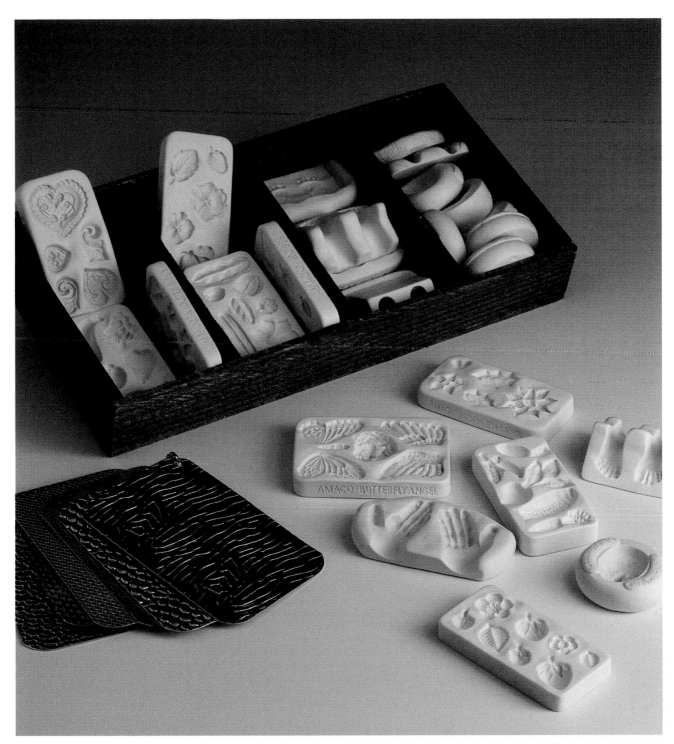

Enjoyment Products Embossing Plates (gold plates with patterns) and American Art Clay Push Molds.

mer clay molds made commercially by companies like the American Art Clay Company that are expressly made to press clay into, remove, then bake. Metal cabochon molds, made by Enjoyment Products Company, can be baked in the oven with the polymer clay

in it. Remember, though, if you bake clay in a metal mold, the shine on the inside of the mold will transfer to the clay (this can be a plus if you want your piece to be shiny and you don't want to buff or coat the clay).

   Some polymer clay molds are not meant

to be baked in the oven. Raw polymer is not usually baked in a baked polymer mold, because it is difficult to release the clay once it has been baked. Therefore, before you press raw clay into the mold, dust it lightly with powder or spray a fine mist of water in the mold. This will help release the clay easily when you are ready. If your mold has deep or pointy crevices, twist the raw clay into a point, press this point into the crevice first, and fit the rest of the clay into the mold evenly, pressing the air bubbles out as you go.

IMITATION: THE BEST FORM OF FLATTERY

Polymer clay is a wonderful medium to use with faux and imitative techniques. As our limited natural resources make buying the real thing either too expensive or next to impossible, these techniques have become increasingly popular. Plastics have helped the environment in that they have slowed the slaughter of animals and trees and the mining of semiprecious minerals for large commercial applications (marble floors, walls, and so on). While a discussion of faux techniques is beyond the scope of this chapter, Tory Hughes has a number of videos on the market that show you exactly how to achieve great faux looks from polymer clay (see Resources on page 89).

GENERAL RULES FOR BAKING POLYMER CLAY

Always read the manufacturer's baking instructions on the package before baking any brand of polymer clay. After that, consider the following general guidelines:

Never bake the clay in a microwave oven. Bake in a toaster oven, conventional oven, or convection oven.

Always bake at the manufacturer's recommended baking temperature or, as I do, 5 to 10 degrees below that temperature to prevent scorching or burning. (If you use the lower temperature, be sure to bake the piece a little longer.) Use an oven thermometer to verify the oven temperature.

Unless otherwise instructed by the manufacturer, bake for 20 to 30 minutes per $\frac{1}{4}$ inch of thickness, and leave the items in the oven to cool once you have turned the oven off. Use a timer to help you keep a careful watch on time.

Place small objects or ones that are well supported with an armature in a heated oven; prop larger objects that may droop solidly with aluminum foil props, and place them in a cold oven.

Make sure that your item is baked properly. Do not assume that baking at a lower temperature for a longer period of time is sufficient to polymerize the item. If the temperature is too low, the polymer molecules will not adhere to one another and, while the outside may appear done, the inside will be brittle, crumbly, or gummy. If your item displays little or no resistance to breakage, falls apart, or feels brittle once it has cooled and you've removed it from the oven, there's a good chance that the item has not been properly baked.

WHAT TO BAKE ON

Most clays darken only slightly after baking, and the more translucent the color the darker the clays end up. Cernit, the most translucent, darkens the most. The more opaque colors of Sculpey III and PROMAT do not darken noticeably. You can bake your polymer clay project on an old Pyrex cake pan, lined with baking parchment or 100 percent rag bond paper. (The less-expensive typing and computer papers with high acid or pulp content tend to scorch, causing the clays to become discolored or to stick to the paper.)

Do not bake on printed materials, such as newspaper or magazine pages, because the print will bake into the clay. (This is quite desirable when it's intentional, but when it's not, it can be disastrous.) Magazine pages tend to be glossy and will actually stick to your clay, but even when they are "unstuck" they will emboss your clay with a shiny spot, resulting from the coating on the paper.

Waxed paper is fine for storing and wrapping your unused clay, but avoid baking on it. It will stick and have the same effect as the magazine pages. Plain brown paper bags are fine, as long as they lie flat and have no obvious seams, wrinkles, or holes. Remember: Because polymer clay picks up absolutely everything, your baking surface should be clean and have roughly the same "texture" as the clay itself.

While none of the projects in this book

deals with bead making, you should keep the following in mind: When baking beads, suspend the beads using a bamboo skewer or a 16-gauge wire from the sides of your baking dish, to prevent them from developing flat or shiny spots and from touching the baking surface. When baking round-bottomed items with no hole (such as a polymer clay-covered egg), you must devise a way to hold the object without denting, scratching, distorting, or flattening the object. Consider baking in a "nest," as Jack Johnston suggests in his book *The Art of Making and Marketing Art Dolls*. He devised a nest of soft material (polyfiber fill) to place his doll heads into while baking, to prevent the dreaded "flat spot." I prefer using wool roving, because polyfiber fill can burn or melt. Make a holder for the roving out of aluminum foil, large enough to hold the object with a lot of extra room. Make the bottom flat and shape sides to hold the wool. Press a hank of wool into the bottom of the foil and

CHART 4 AVERAGE POLYMER BAKING TEMPERATURES

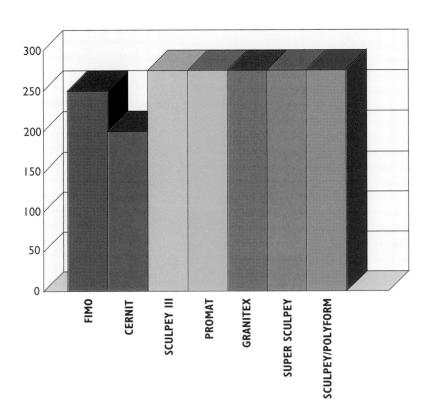

make a nest with your hand, indenting an area large enough to accommodate your object. Bake as usual.

WHICH GLUES TO USE

There are a number of glues on the market. They are made from a variety of materials: common substances (wheat paste), complex chemical bonds (cyanoacrylate ester, or super glue), melted plastic (hot glue), dairy products (Elmer's), and silicone or caulk (GOOP). There are even two-part glues that have a base and a catalyst to create a strong bonding reaction, such as two-part epoxies.

With so many glues to choose from, which one do you select for your project? Generally, the more chemical the bond the more it will stick to cured (baked) polymer clay. Neither hot glue nor Elmer's (nor Tacky Glue) last and, in my experience, they eventually peel off. Wheat paste simply flakes off. Two-part epoxies are messy, have an odor, and are too much of a bother for most people. Many super glues are finicky and some brands do not hold well at all or have mixed results—that is, the bond fails over time. However, Loctite is a well-known high-quality super glue that creates a stronger bond than its less-expensive imitators. Loctite glues go by the names Quick Tite or Creatively Yours. Another excellent glue is GOOP—and it can be Craftsmen's Goop, AMACO's Friendly Plastic Arts and Crafts GOOP, or E 6000. They all have essentially the same glue base, just a different moniker. A word of caution about super glues: Keep acetone around to unstick your fingers in case you accidentally glue them together; if the acetone doesn't work, flush the area with water and call a doctor. Do not scratch near your eyes, nose, or lips while using the glue, and be sure to remove all glue residue from your fingertips when you are finished.

Use GOOP and Loctite's liquid super glue in a well-ventilated area. Do not inhale or sniff the fumes from these products because they can be damaging, even deadly. If you believe you are pregnant, avoid handling these products and have someone else glue your items for you.

To this point, I have only talked about gluing cured (baked) items. In many of the projects in this book, I use raw (unbaked) clay that needs to be adhered to the surface it is layered on, without the possibility of it shifting or peeling up from the surface. Polymer clay is an adaptable substance that will readily adhere to a smooth oil or dust-free surface, such as glass, metal, and certain plastics. But, there are other surfaces that the clay can't adhere to because it can't get a good enough grip, usually those that are pebbly or porous (for example, cardboard, wood, and unglazed ceramic). In these cases, two brands of glue work especially well: Loctite liquid super glue and Sobo white craft and fabric glue. There are advantages and disadvantages to each.

Loctite Liquid Super Glue

If there is a difference in the two types of Loctite glues, Quiktite and Creatively Yours, I can't tell it in my work. The formulation seems to be essentially the same, if not identical.

To apply super glue to your polymer clay:

1. Be sure the surface that you are gluing the clay to is clean, dry, and free of oil and dust. If needed, rough up the surface a bit with steel wool or medium-grit sandpaper, and clean well with a damp clean cloth. Do not sand the brown papier-mâché items, unless it is necessary to remove a bump; in so doing you can create a bigger mess that it's worth. Also, don't overly wet the surface; this will cause it to peel. Simply clean the object lightly with a damp cloth and allow the surface to dry completely before gluing.

(Beginners may wish to cut patterns from the clay a quarter-inch to a half-inch larger than the edges of the project, so you have room to play if you mistakenly mis-align the clay.)

2.   Work one small section at a time, especially on larger projects. A little liquid super glue will go a long way when spread thinly with a small icing spatula or palette knife, but remember that this glue dries quickly. If you are working with a flat area, such as a papier-mâché box lid or frame, start applying the glue at one edge; then spread the glue thinly and evenly around with your spatula. (Be sure to keep a cloth handy and immediately clean the spatula, or you'll get a build-up of glue on it.) Work quickly while the glue is still wet to lay the *already cut* clay onto the surface, gluing only a few inches at a time. Other-wise, the glue will set-up (dry) before you get the clay applied properly. When applied in a thin layer, the glue has an "open time" of only two to three minutes before it dries.

3.   It is important to align the clay at least along that glued edge first and press it down from that edge. Press gently and evenly, to eliminate the air bubbles beneath the surface. Smooth the clay downward (away from the edge you are gluing), releasing the air bubbles as you press. Press firmly, yet not so firmly as to distort your clay, especially if smoothness is the desired end result. When you have reached the end of the glue line, *gently* fold the clay backward onto itself. It may help to insert a piece of rolled typing paper between the two surfaces if your clay is sticky. (The "rolled" edge will be placed at the point at which the clay is folded back-ward onto itself.)

4.   Apply more glue, spreading evenly as before, and repeat the above steps.

5.   Continue to work the clay over the surface to smooth it out, slice sideways into any bubbles you may detect, and gently press in the direction of the slice. (Avoid

piercing the bubble from the top: You may create a hole that's difficult to get rid of and you may not be able to eliminate all of the air, anyway!)

6.   Bake as directed in the project, or according to the clay manufacturer's directions.

Sobo

Sobo is billed as a "premium craft and fab-ric glue." It is a thick, white, non-yellowing water-based glue that looks and smells like many other white glues. It is water-soluble (which means it's easy to clean up with soap and water) and it dries quickly when spread thinly. It works well to adhere poly-mer clay to porous/semiporous surfaces, such as papier-mâché and cardboard. It has the AP-certified nontoxic seal, making it the glue to use when "claying" with young children. Best of all, it's great for those larger projects because it's inexpensive.

When applying Sobo, I use the following technique:

1.   Be sure that the surface you are gluing the clay to is clean, dry, and free of oil and dust. If needed, rough up the sur-face a bit with steel wool or medium-grit sandpaper, and clean well with a damp clean cloth. Do not sand the brown papier-mâché items unless it is necessary to remove a bump; in so doing you can create a bigger mess that it's worth. Also, don't overly wet the surface, because this will cause it to peel. Simply clean the object lightly with a damp cloth and allow the surface to dry completely before gluing.

2.   Use a small icing spatula or palette knife to spread the glue. Be generous in applying it, and spread the clay thinly and evenly. Because Sobo is rather tacky, it is more difficult to spread, but as long as the glue is uniformly applied, you don't have to worry about the surface of the glue looking perfect; it won't. Cover the entire surface of the project area to which you are applying

the clay. The clay can then be applied to wet or tacky Sobo.

3. Smooth the clay downward (away from the edge you are gluing), releasing the air bubbles as you press. Press firmly, yet not so firmly as to distort your clay, especially if smoothness is the desired end result. When you have reached the end of the glue line, *gently* fold the clay backward onto itself. It may help to insert a piece of rolled typing paper between the two surfaces if your clay is sticky. (The "rolled" edge will be placed at the point at which the clay is folded backward onto itself.)

4. Continue to work the clay over the surface to smooth it out, slice sideways into any bubbles you may detect, and gently press in the direction of the slice. (Avoid piercing the bubble from the top: You may create a hole that's difficult to get rid of and you may not be able to eliminate all of the air, anyway!)

5. Bake as directed in the project, or according to the clay manufacturer's directions.

A Word of Safety

Because clay forms the top layer of what you're baking, the clay, not the glue, gives off the fumes, or the odor you normally smell when you're baking these projects. But, you may still wonder whether the glue gives off noxious fumes when it is baked or whether hazardous chemical reactions occur between the polymer and the glue during the baking process. According to my research, there is no known danger in baking a water-based nontoxic white glue like Sobo or super glues like Loctite, because they break down at about 350 degrees, not the temperature at which you are baking your projects.

When baking polymer clay, it is important to bake in a well-ventilated area. (Manufacturers tell you that their products were never intended for production

baking, which in my estimation is anything over an hour or so a day.) Try baking in your garage, or vent your toaster oven outdoors with the hood fan above your range. If you are lucky enough to live in a warmer climate, bake outdoors on the picnic table or porch.

The Definition of Finish

"Patina" usually means the way a surface looks in any given state. When I refer to patina in this book I am talking about polymer brands after baking—that is, the natural postbaked, nontampered look, feel, and finish. For example, copper has many patinas: If it is unmined and in the raw state, it is both reddish gold and green in color. In its mined and newly forged state, it is a bright red color, but with no surface shine. When it is buffed, the color stays essentially the same (a little less red, perhaps) and the finish feels smooth and has a very bright and glassy shine. If left to the elements, it oxidizes and, in time, turns a greenish gray blotchy color with hints of red. The surface develops a scaly feel and looks dull again.

Polyform clays like Sculpey III, Polyform/Sculpey, and Granitex all have a dull patina. This does not mean, however, that the colors are dull or not as bright as FIMO, whose patina is more waxy-looking, or Glamour Cernit, whose patina looks most shiny or semigloss. An added patina is a substance, finish, or method of polishing or adding another finish, such as lacquer. Gold and silver leafing fall under this patina category. It is an embedded substance that becomes one with the clay and adds a new look to the final color, feel, and finish.

Added Finishes

Even though many people prefer the look of unfinished (natural) polymer clay, there are various types of lacquers and varnishes that are compatible with the clay and can be applied to enhance its look.

"Why do I need to apply a finish at all?" Well, you really don't. Obviously, you don't need to "protect" the piece from marring, as you would a piece of fine wood furniture. I have intentionally not used lacquers or varnishes in any of the projects in this book, although if you love the glossy look, use the gloss-finished lacquer. If your aim is to intensify the color of the clay somewhat, but not add shine, then the matte lacquer may be what you wish to apply.

Eberhard Faber

There are several finishes available from Eberhard Faber that are specially formulated for use on cured polymer clay. Some are petroleum based and some are water based. The petroleum-based have color-coded caps (black for the gloss varnish and red for the matte varnish) and may require thinning (if so, use paint thinner). Use a solvent-based cleaner such as turpentine, turpenoid, or an oil-dissolving odorless brush cleaner. Of course, use caution with these products. Good ventilation is a must, as well as a no smoking policy, when applying the lacquer and cleaners.

The water-based finishes also have color-coded caps (green for the matte varnish and blue for the gloss varnish). These lacquers clean up with soap and water, are virtually odorless, and dry quickly. I recommend good ventilation, anyway, just as a precaution. I have a very sensitive nose, but good ventilation should be a rule when using any chemical.

The best method for applying these lacquers depends upon the project. Like all varnishes and lacquers, you must apply it to clean, dry (baked) clay with a sponge brush or a very soft bristle brush. Apply in thin, even coats. When dry to the touch, reapply.

Additional Options

I've found that Delta's water-based varnishes work very well on polymer clay. These include an exterior that dries with a nice

glossy finish, a matte all-purpose finish, a gloss all-purpose finish, and a semigloss all-purpose finish. Each comes in a convenient flip-top 2-ounce plastic squeeze bottle. There are also other spray brands that work well with the polymers. Carnival Arts Ultraglaze works well with polymer clay and Krylon's matte spray coating works well if you only spray a very light single coat on your piece.

Some sprays and finishes react with the clay and seem to remain tacky to the touch forever. I contend that a small amount of plasticizer residue may remain on the clays and possibly some may leach out, causing a reaction between the clay and the finish. Unless you know a great deal about the compatibility of these products with polymers, it is best not to experiment; otherwise, test the finish on a piece you do not care about. If possible, test before you buy. With hand polishing and buffing, fine sanding and dremels, it is usually better to choose the natural unglazed methods available if you're in doubt. It looks better, is more environmentally responsible, and will add value to your finished piece.

One finishing option I have not yet mentioned is Johnson's paste wax. You can wax your items to a lovely warm buttery finish, simply by using the wax as you would when you wax your car. Dip a finger in, press a small amount of wax onto the surface of your piece, and spread it around in small circles until the wax "melts." Let it dry for about a half hour; then buff with a soft cloth, muslin buffing wheel, or Dremel. Spray furniture polish works very well, also, and Future floor wax liquid also works great.

CLEAN-UP AND STORAGE

One of the terrific things about polymer clay is that it is so clean to work with (besides a stray crumb or two that may flip off your work area onto the floor). Most of the clays have minimal bleeding or staining. The reds in all the brands cling to your hands the most easily, so be sure to clean your hands between colors, especially if you go from red to a lighter color. A good rule of thumb is to start with the lightest colors in your design, then progress to the next darker, and so on. I still like to clean up between colors so that I do not contaminate one color with another.

There are many simple methods for cleaning up between colors and after you have finished your work for the day. These methods do not involve expensive cleaners or involved processes. Keep a large economy-sized bottle of inexpensive hand cream at your work area as well as several old clean terry-cloth or rough rags, isopropyl alcohol, and baby wipes.

Begin by cleaning your work area before you use it. Soak a large area of a clean rag with alcohol. Swab the area you will be working on and finish by drying it with the dry part of the rag. Set the rag unfolded, over your pasta machine or draped on something the alcohol won't soak into, so it will dry. Next, after you have washed your hands, condition them with a dab of lotion. Rub your hands together, and let the lotion soak in; then you are ready to work with your first batch of clay.

Once you have completed your first color, clean your hands using a generous dollop of hand lotion, and wipe with the clean terry-cloth rags, as if you were washing with liquid hand soap, but don't rinse it off. The hand lotion will act as a soaplike agent, breaking down the layer of oil and polymer on your hands. Clean between colors this way until your project is finished. Not only will your hands be relatively clean, but they will be very soft. After you have added the last detail to your project and you are ready to call it quits for the day, "wash" your hands once more using the lotion, then wash with cool water and a good hand soap. If your hands

still have an oily feel, follow with an isopropyl alcohol rinse. Splash a bit of it into a clean rag and scrub your hands until they feel dry and oil-free. If needed, apply the lotion one last time, and your hands should feel as if you just had a professional massage.

The alcohol will not overdry your hands, because it is used only once or twice a day, at final clean-up time. Do not use the alcohol before you wash with soap, however; there is some debate that this drives the polymer into your skin, which you don't want. Wash the rags in hot soapy water by hand or separately in the washer with bleach and a good detergent. Hanging them out to dry not only freshens them but makes them a little rougher, so they actually absorb more polymer and lotion next time around. You can avoid this clean-up altogether by wearing inexpensive latex gloves, sold at your local pharmacy. Just toss them once they're worn or too contaminated with color.

CLEANING YOUR PASTA MACHINE

When you start to see traces of other colors in your clay as you run it through the pasta machine, you know that it's time to clean your machine. Undo the machine from its table clamp, turn it over, and examine the underside around the rollers. You will see an accumulation of clay clinging to the plate under the roller edges. There may also be a line of clay at the edge of the blades. Take an old soft toothbrush and scrape off what you can; then insert an old rag into the machine and scrape off the clay from around the rollers. (This will be difficult, because it's a very tight fit.) If you do this often enough (once a week if you are a heavy "user"), it will keep the "crud" from accumulating and contaminating your clean clay as you roll it through.

You may also want to swab the outside with a little isopropyl alcohol on an old clean rag to clean the oily polymer residue off of the machine. (However, *never use water*. The water will rust the blades, making them difficult to turn or ruining them so they never turn again.) I also like to turn the handle while running the same alcohol-dampened rag over the rollers. *I do not recommend dismantling the machine!* It is usually not necessary, and it is very difficult to put the machine back together once you have taken it apart. If you make a habit of cleaning often, you will never have to take it apart.

STORING YOUR POLYMER CLAY

The best method for storing polymer clay is placing it away from a direct or constant indirect heat source and away from ultraviolet light. Heat and ultraviolet light, or sunlight, prematurely age polymer clay. I have a section reserved in my refrigerator for my FIMO and Cernit. (Cernit tends to be even more heat-sensitive than FIMO.) It's cool and away from any sunlight. I store my new, unconditioned clay in covered plastic see-through tubs in my refrigerator and freezer. Sculpey III is the least affected by the heat, and it seems as if its shelf life is indeterminable.

Conditioned clay that I will use within the month, I roll into long thin sheets (through the pasta machine on setting three), sandwich between layers of waxed paper, and store away from heat and sunlight. Conditioned clay that I will use at a later time, I store in the refrigerator because heat cures the clay quicker when it is stored in thin sheets. Also keep in mind that FIMO stiffens up in its conditioned state sooner than any of the other brands and involves more conditioning if it is not used within a week or two.

CHAPTER FOUR

WORKING WITH COLOR

MARBLEIZING

One of polymer clay's most exciting properties is its extensive color range. Anyone can create custom colors just by knowing the "secrets" of mixing colors.

Marbleizing is the first step in mixing colors using polymer clay. The process of marbleizing is like mixing paint, only the "paint" is solid. What happens when you drop a small amount of black paint into a large amount of white paint and swirl it around? At first, you get a black dot in a pool of white. As you manipulate the black and blend it with the white, the colors marbleize. As you continue to mix and the paints converge, the swirls begin to dissipate, but a definite swirl pattern of white against black evolves. The white overpowers the black as the black molecules move farther and farther apart, ending up a light gray. This is exactly what happens with polymer clay. Therefore, if you know anything about color mixing with paint, you already know almost everything about mixing color with polymer clay. Marbleization is just the preliminary phase of full-color blending.

Marbleization sounds and looks exotic, but it's a beginner's paradise, because it's easy to achieve beautiful results. When I started experimenting with polymer clay, I remember becoming enthralled with the patterns and swirls of color I could create,

simply by mixing, moving, and manipulating two colors together.

There are shortcuts, tips, and hints to becoming an adept polymer clay color mixer. Work the clays you wish to combine by hand until they are well conditioned and pliable. Crumbly clay does not work well with this process because the crumbles do not marbleize thoroughly and take a long time to mix if you haven't done the preliminary conditioning.

COLOR MIXING

Progressing from black-and-white marbleization to color mixing is like stepping from the simple, predictable, and easy into the confusing and immense. However, it doesn't have to be so overwhelming because the same basic color mixing rules that apply to paint apply to polymer clay. When you blend a small amount of black with a larger amount of white, you get light gray; when you add a tiny bit of red to a large amount of white, you get pink. This type of color blending is called *tinting* (Fig. 4-1). Eliminate the white and instead add black to a color and you have a *shade* (Fig. 4-2). Mix any color with gray and you create a *tone* (Fig. 4-3).

Primary colors are the three basic colors on the color wheel: red, blue, and yellow (Fig. 4-4). By mixing two primary colors together, you create *secondary colors*, such

FIG. 4-1 MIXING TINTS

FIG. 4-2 MIXING SHADES

FIG. 4-3 MIXING TONES

FIG. 4-4 PRIMARY COLOR CHART

FIG. 4-5 SECONDARY COLOR CHART

FIG. 4-6 MIXING CHART FOR SECONDARY COLORS

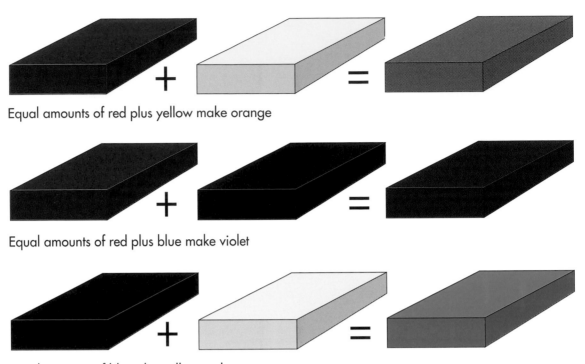

Equal amounts of red plus yellow make orange

Equal amounts of red plus blue make violet

Equal amounts of blue plus yellow make green

as green, orange, and violet (Fig. 4-5). To get these secondaries, mix the following colors: red + yellow, red + blue, yellow + blue, and so on (Fig. 4-6). By mixing a primary color and a secondary color, you end up with a *tertiary color* (for example, red + orange, blue + green, and so on). Add equal amounts of yellow, blue, and red and you get a brownish purple; add a little less blue and the brown becomes richer and less gray; add a little less red and the color becomes more gray-green.

There are also *intermediary colors*, which you can create by mixing primary colors and secondary colors. Intermediaries include yellow-orange, red-orange, red-violet, blue-violet, blue-green, and yellow-green. The combinations are endless and you can create an incredible range of shades simply by adjusting the color ratios.

There are many useful books on color and you can relate the information directly to mixing your own custom colors using polymer clay.* While colors vary from man-

ufacturer to manufacturer (FIMO's carmine red is nothing like Sculpey III's maroon, yet they are both red.), remember that one-half block of red mixed with one-half block of yellow will always yield orange, regardless of the brand—and the same holds true when mixing other polymer clay colors.

*Margaret Maggio, The Color Column, January–May 1996 issues of the National Polymer Clay Guild's newsletter, The PolyInformer.

FULL-COLOR MIXING METHODS

The mechanics of color mixing by hand are simple. As outlined under marbleizing, condition the clay, form the two conditioned colors into snakes, and roll and twist them together until fully blended, creating another color. If your clay is hard or stubborn or if you need to mix a large amount of clay, you can quickly mix the colors together with a food processor. If you are using FIMO, this method relieves the stress and fatigue your hands and arms can encounter during arduous mixing sessions involving large amounts of clay.

Beginners should start by mixing small amounts of clay, noting the ratios that they use (for example, 1/8 ounce white to 1/16 ounce blue makes X color). Cut a small chip, bake it, and mount it on your color chart for easy reference, this way you will always know what ratios you need to re-create your colors. If you need to make larger amounts, just do some simple math: If you used 1/2 ounce red to 2 ounces white to make your favorite pink and you need to double that amount, you need 1 ounce red to 4 ounces white.

To condition and mix large amounts of clay, break the clay into small chunks, about the size of small cheese cubes. Drop a few at a time into the chute of your food processor as the blades are turning, *but remember to keep your fingers out of the chute.* The clay will either resemble coffee grounds or cottage cheese, depending on the amount of plasticizer the clay had in it when you dropped it in. The drier the clay, the finer the granules will be. Once the first color is well blended, add the second color, allowing the machine to warm the clay as it blends. Once the two colors are well distributed, stop the machine. If the granules look like coffee grounds, you may need to add a couple tiny drops of hand lotion to the bowl and remix. When the clay begins to hold together, it will be softer and easier to mix and condition by hand.

Dump the mixed clay onto your work surface and pat any stray pieces together into a ball with your hands. Roll them together, making a snake. This will begin the blending process. Keep kneading, twisting, and folding the snake until the colors are fully blended and form a completely mixed color.

Softer clays like Cernit or Sculpey III usually do not need to be conditioned with a food processor; they are generally easy to blend by hand or with the help of a pasta machine. When using the pasta machine to blend, keep the following tips in mind:

- Knead the colors together into a marbleized state before inserting the clay into the pasta machine.

- Turn and fold the clay in opposite directions each time and put the clay into the blades folded end first. This not only eliminates air bubbles, but the constant folding and turning blends the colors quicker and more efficiently.

Now, you can create colorful and innovative works of art. If you have read carefully up to this point, you are armed with the knowledge it has taken many artists years of failures, successes, and experimentation to achieve. Now, let's make some projects!

Part Two

POLYMER CLAY

PROJECTS

CHOCOLATE SWEETS FOR THE DIETER

WARNING! *These candies look so convincingly real that someone may try to eat one. Keep them away from tempted hands and mouths, especially children's, by putting them in a sealed glass display jar on a high shelf or instead making them into lapel pins, scatter pins, mini tree decorations, package decorations, or refrigerator magnets.*

Skill level: Beginner
Yield: one dozen pieces of faux candy

MATERIALS

- FIMO: 2 ounces terra-cotta (FIMO is the only clay that comes in this color!)
- Food processor (optional)
- Plastic candy molds of your choice
- Small thin round brush
- Talcum, cosmetic, or baby powder to dust the inside of the molds
- Freezer/refrigerator to put the filled molds in
- Old clean terry-cloth rag
- Baking parchment or rag bond paper
- Oven
- Pastel acrylic paints

STEP 1. Condition the clay until it is smooth, shiny, and crumble-free, using a food processor, if necessary.

STEP 2. Dust the insides of the candy molds thoroughly with talcum, cosmetic, or baby powder, using a small thin round brush.

STEP 3. Roll a ball out of the terra-cotta clay about the size of the mold. Press firmly into the mold, making sure that all of the crevices are tightly filled and that there are no visible gaps or air bubbles through the clear plastic.

STEP 4. Once you've filled all the molds with clay, place them in the freezer for ten minutes. This solidifies the clay and creates a slight water vapor between the clay, the talc, and the mold, making it easier to release the clay from the mold.

STEP 5. Carefully pull the flexible plastic edge of the mold slightly away from the clay. You will see an air pocket develop inside the mold where the clay is releasing. It will pop out of the mold eventually, so don't pry it out with a tool, or you may damage the "candy." If the mold is deep or intricate, you can insert a toothpick into the center of the clay and pull the clay out. Carefully dust off any excess talc sticking to the clay with the terry-cloth rag.

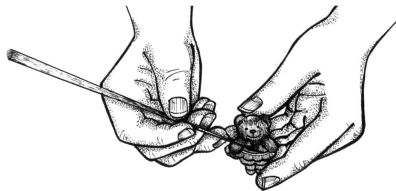

STEP 6. Bake the candy on a sheet of baking parchment at the manufacturer's baking temperature for one hour. Allow to cool in oven before removing it. Decorate each piece with pastel acrylic paints.

GRANDMA'S OLD-FASHIONED "NO-CAL" SUGAR COOKIES

Use these adorable faux cookies to decorate mini and regular-sized Christmas trees.

Skill level: Beginner
Yield: Six figures

MATERIALS

I used white PROMAT in this project to give my cookies more strength, but you can use regular white Sculpey III if you don't have PROMAT or if strength is not a factor.

- PROMAT: 1 ounce white
  (or FIMO: 1 ounce champagne) $^1/_4$ ounce red

- Sculpey III: 2 ounces tan intermediate
  $^1/_4$ ounce yellow pearl

- Food processor (optional)

- Pasta machine

- Wilton cookie or canapé cutters in various shapes: gingerbread people, teddy bears, stars, Christmas trees, and angels

- Old clean terry-cloth rag

- Brownish tan powdered blush, face powder, or eye shadow

- Small soft round brush

- Kemper tools/pattern cutters: Heart cutter pch 7, circle cutter pcr 5, flower cutter pcf 7, pro tool

- Two black seed beads

- Stylus

- Loctite liquid super glue

- FISKARS Paper Edgers scissors for cutting trim on angel dress

- Baking parchment or rag bond paper

- Oven

STEP 1. Condition the clay, using a food processor, if necessary. Mix 1 ounce white clay to 2 ounces tan, or use champagne FIMO. Flatten the clay by rolling it through the pasta machine on setting three, until it is approximately $^1/_8$ inch thick. Use your choice of cookie cutters to cut shapes.

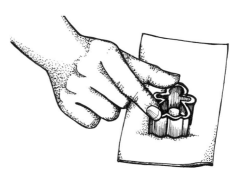

STEP 2. Press/dab the terry-cloth rag randomly into the clay's surface, paying close attention to the edges, pressing them a little harder than the rest of the cookie so you lose that hard-edged look. You want to achieve a lightly textured sugar cookie look, so be

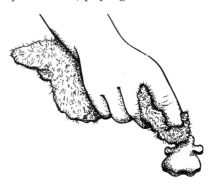

sure that you are not stroking the rag onto the surface. Once satisfied with the texture, you can embellish the cookies or leave them plain.

STEP 3. To get that nicely browned look of home-baked sugar cookies, apply a brownish tan powdered blush, face powder, or eye shadow to the edges of the cookies with a soft round brush. Use up-and-down dabbing motions. Don't stroke the powder on—it will streak the surface. Once you're satisfied with the results, dab the edges lightly with the

terry-cloth rag. It is important that you dab here, because stroking will ruin your hard work by leaving streaks in the cookies.

STEP 4. To embellish the gingerbread people: Cut three candy buttons for each figure from the red clay, using the Kemper heart cutter; once baked, buff slightly to obtain a candy-like sheen.

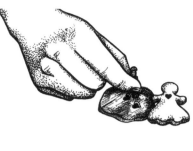

STEP 5. For the hair, wrap a tiny yellow snake of clay loosely around the tip of the pro tool, similar to a tendril but

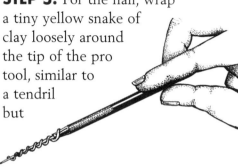

tighter together, more like a coil. Slip the clay off the end of the needle and press it onto the top of the head: Gingerboy has three loops, gingergirl eight.

STEP 6. Create eyes by pressing two black seed beads securely into the surface of the clay with the stylus, to prevent the eyes from falling out. (A touch of super glue will hold the eyes in if they drop out after baking.)

STEP 7. Cut out two cheeks for each figure from the red clay, using the Kemper circle cutter, and press them securely into the surface of the clay. Once you've placed the cheeks on, etch a smile into the face with the pro tool. Once baked, buff slightly to obtain a candy-like sheen.

STEP 8. Create the candy cane by lightly marbleizing red and white clay together

and then twisting. Roll a snake, approximately ½ inch long by ⅛ inch in diameter.

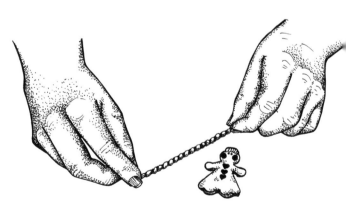

Bend the end and press it onto the body.

parchment or rag bond paper). Bake at 265 degrees for forty-five minutes; then let them cool in the oven before removing.

Full Size Template

Angels, Stars, Teddy Bears, and Christmas Trees

Follow the above general directions. Use the appropriate cookie cutter or trace the provided pattern, place it on the flattened clay, and cut out the shape. Texture as described using the clean, terry-cloth rag. Embellish with your choice of stars, hearts, beads, or FISKARS Paper Edger scissor trimmings. Make several cookies at one time (enough to fill a cookie sheet lined with baking

TIP: To make thicker cookies, double the clay's thickness by folding sheet of clay in half after running it through the pasta machine on setting one; then cut shapes with cutters as directed.

Ideas

Use these adorable faux cookies to decorate mini and regular-sized Christmas trees (just poke a hole in the top with the pro tool or needle tool before baking so you can string them with thin satin ribbon and hang them). Add to wreaths or packages (print "To," "From," and appropriate info on it as a gift tag), or place them in the Christmas tree box you just made (see "Christmas Tree Box" on page 82). Make them into adorable lapel pins, "Baby's First Christmas" ornaments, or even set them out where children aren't tempted to nibble on them—on a plate for Santa! You could also add a note that the cookies have no fat, no sugar, no cholesterol, and no calories. Bon appetit, Santa!

INTERNET INK PEN

To give your pens a richer look and some added surface texture, roll gold leaf or silver leaf into the clay before baking.

Skill level: Beginner

MATERIALS

- Friendly Cay, Cernit, FIMO, or PROMAT or a mixture of two or more clays (to make a random-patterned pen):
  1 ounce of the color of your choice
- Bic Round Stic pen (imitation brands will melt in the oven)
- Pliers
- One sheet wet/dry sandpaper, medium grit
- Clean damp rag to wipe your pen between sandings
- Food processor (optional)
- Pasta machine
- Tissue slicer
- X-ACTO knife
- Baking parchment or rag bond paper
- Oven
- One sheet automotive-finish sandpaper, 1,500 grit (optional)
- One sheet wet/dry sand-paper, fine 600 grit (optional)
- Large bowl of water to sand your pen in (optional)
- Dremel Mototool with a muslin buffing wheel or buffer/grinder with muslin buff (optional)

STEP 1. Remove the ink cartridge from the barrel of the pen by gently twisting and pulling the metal band (located below the plastic collar and above the metal point) with pliers. Set the cartridge aside.

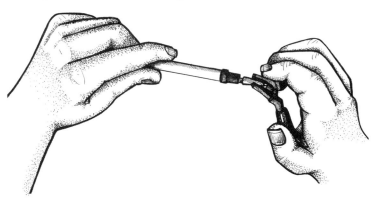

STEP 2. Thoroughly sand the barrel of the pen with the medium-grit sandpaper; then wipe with a clean damp cloth, so that the clay will adhere to it better. Condition your clay, using the food processor, if needed, and roll it through the pasta machine. If you want your pen to have a thick, heavy feel, use setting three; for a thinner, lighter feel, use setting four or five.

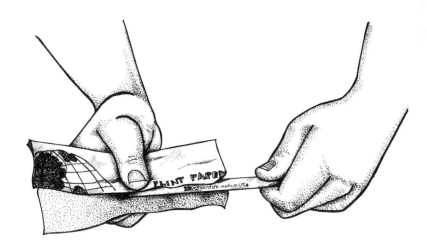

STEP 3. Lay the empty pen barrel onto the sheet of rolled out clay, along one of the edges. Cut a straight edge in the clay with your tissue slicer; then lay the pen onto that straight edge, measure from tip to end, and use your tissue slicer to slice straight vertical cuts perpendicular to the pen.

STEP 4. Setting the extra clay aside, roll the pen toward the opposite end of the clay, making sure that there are no air bubbles trapped beneath the surface. Stretch the clay taut during this process, to ensure fewer air bubbles and a smoother finish. Roll gently until the pen stops rolling easily and is completely covered with clay.

the pen, carefully butting the two cut edges together at the seam.

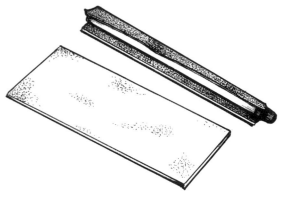

TIP: The stickier the clay in this project, the better. Well-conditioned, sticky clay, such as FIMO and Cernit, works well because it adheres to the pen's surface and reduces the likelihood of trapped air bubbles

STEP 6. Continue to roll the pen on its side until the clay becomes smooth and the seam disappears. Don't worry if the clay extrudes a bit from one of the ends; you can either use it to cover the closed end or trim it with your tissue slicer when you are satisfied with the look of the clay covering.

STEP 5. Gently roll the pen backward until you see a slight line or indentation by the first cut edge of the clay; then cut along this line with your X-ACTO knife. Re-roll the clay over

STEP 7. Using your X-ACTO knife, gently slice into any air bubbles that are trapped inside. (Remember: Don't poke a hole—it will be difficult to repair!) Press the air out and reseal the clay by smoothing and pressing gently.

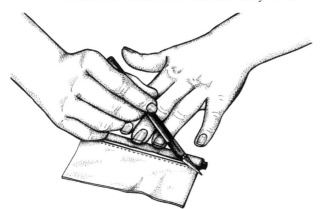

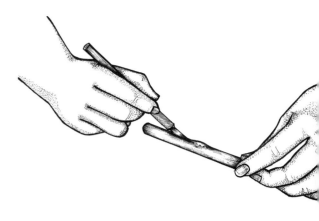

TIP: Leave both ends of the pen "open" until you have released all of the trapped air bubbles, this way you can actually move the bubbles to either open end by pressing them out in one direction of the other.

STEP 8. Smooth out any fingerprints by burnishing—that is, stroking the length of the pen with your index finger until the clay is smooth and shiny. Bake on a sheet of baking parchment or rag bond paper at the manufacturer's baking temperature for thirty minutes. Let it cool in the oven until just warm, about one hour, before removing.

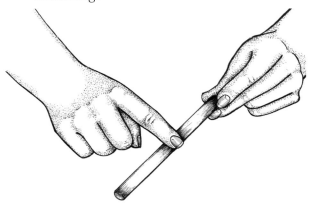

STEP 9. For a high-gloss finish, wet-sand the pen when completely cool with the 600-grit sandpaper. If your pen is bumpy or rough, use the 400-grit paper to sand off the roughness; then use 600-grit paper. Finish with the 1,500-grit paper, if needed. Polish using the Dremel Mototool or Foredom buffing wheel.

STEP 10. Replace the ink cartridge using the pliers.

IDEAS

To give your pens a richer look and some added surface texture, roll gold leaf or silver leaf into the clay before baking. Make faux marble (see Chapter 4), jade, and ivory pens. If you are into canemaking, press cane slices into the clay before baking. Top each pen with a different animal, bug, or object to make critter pens. Add bits of paper, beads, dirt, or anything that can be baked to the surface—the sky's the limit!

"Spicy" Jar Lids

Cover the entire jar with polymer clay, or make a "chili pepper" cane and embellish the outside with that. Make matching polymer-covered chili-pepper handles for a spoon to use with your salsa or 3-D chili-pepper napkin rings—your only limit is your imagination!

Skill level: Intermediate

MATERIALS

- For the Mexican Sombrero Lid—Cernit: 1 ounce glamour yellow, 1/4 ounce caramel, 1/4 ounce leaf green, 1/4 ounce red
- For the Red-Flowered Lid—Cernit: 1/2 ounce yellow no. 1, one package leaf green; PROMAT: one package red, one package black, one package white, one package tomato red
- Food processor (optional)
- Pasta machine
- Chi-Chi's salsa jar and lid
- X-ACTO knife
- Sobo white glue
- Leather Factory tool: Basket-weave tool #X500
- Kemper tools/pattern cutters: Teardrop cutter pc5t, pro tool, circle cutter pcbr, flower cutter pc1r
- Flower-shaped canapé cutters (or use pattern provided to cut freehand) for flower jar lids
- Small soft round brush
- Brown powdered eye shadow
- Baking parchment or rag bond paper
- Oven

MEXICAN SOMBRERO LID

STEP 1. Condition all clays, using the food processor, if needed. Roll the glamour yellow clay through the pasta machine on setting two. Lay the jar lid on top of the clay upside down and cut with your X-ACTO knife around the outside, making your circle slightly larger than the lid. Set this circle aside.

STEP 2. Re-roll the remaining clay through the pasta machine on setting three. Cut a thin strip the width of the edge of the jar lid, about 8 inches long by 1/2 inch wide, and set aside.

STEP 3. Spread a thin, even layer of Sobo glue on the top of the lid; then allow it to dry until tacky. Roll a ball of glamour yellow about 1 inch in diameter and press it to the top center of the lid. The bottom of the ball should naturally flatten out as it touches the lid, but also flare the bottom out slightly to make it look like the crown of a hat. Smooth all bumps and slice into any air bubbles with your X-ACTO knife.

STEP 4. Center the circle of clay that you set aside in step one over the top of the lid, stretching as you lay it over the center ball of clay. Smooth the bumps as you go by

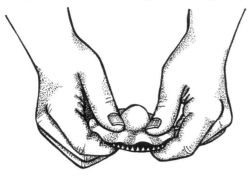

pressing gently toward the outside edge. Be sure the top layer of clay makes firm contact with the metal of the lid; slice into any air bubbles with your X-ACTO knife.

STEP 5. Spread Sobo glue thinly and evenly over the open edge of the lid and allow it to dry until tacky. Press the strip you set aside in step two to the edge, smoothing with your fingertips, and blend this edge into the top edge of the hat brim.

STEP 6. Texture the crown and the brim of the hat using the Leather Factory basket-weave tool, starting at the center of the crown and working downward.

TIP: It helps to rock the tool in place gently from end to end to complete a full impression of the pattern. You may wish to practice this texturing technique on a separate sheet of clay before you tackle the hat.

STEP 7. Roll two thin snakes of caramel clay, each measuring about 5 inches long by $1/16$ inch in diameter.

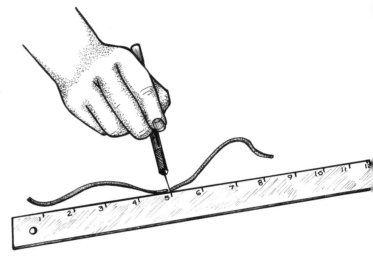

STEP 8. Twist the two together and wrap them around the hat where the crown meets the brim. Tie them in a "knot" and fray the ends by slicing several times with your X-ACTO knife.

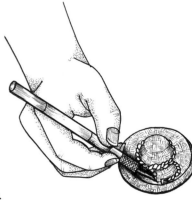

STEP 9. Roll the leaf green clay through the pasta machine on setting four, cut nine small leaves using the Kemper teardrop pattern cutter, and arrange them in a random trailing pattern on the crown and brim. Press the pro tool into the length of each leaf to create a vein and to secure the leaf in place.

TIP: Be sure to leave some space for those chili peppers!

STEP 10. Roll a snake from the red clay, approximately 4 inches long by ⅛ inch in diameter. Cut five "logs" from the snake, each about ¾ inch long. Taper each end to a point, twist slightly, add some divots and indentations with your fingers, and press onto the crown.

STEP 11. Using the small soft round brush, lightly and carefully dust the hat with the brown powdered eye shadow Be sure not to dust the chili peppers or leaves! Bake on a sheet of baking parchment or rag bond paper at the manufacturer's baking temperature for forty-five minutes; then allow to cool in oven before removing. If desired, once cool, carefully buff the chili peppers to a gloss with a soft clean rag.

Note: I have used this jar lid extensively at home. It has been in and out of the refrigerator and on and off the jar many times—and it has survived beautifully! Just hand wash in dish detergent with the rest of your dishes and dry with a soft towel. You can either refill/recycle the salsa jar, or you can buy another jar and reuse your Mexican Sombrero Lid on it!

Red-Flowered Lid

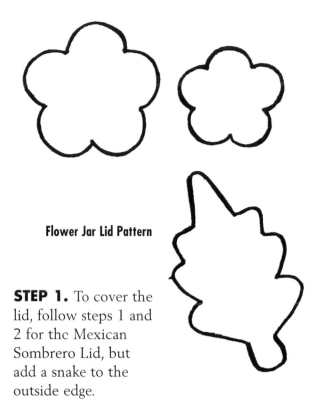

Flower Jar Lid Pattern

STEP 1. To cover the lid, follow steps 1 and 2 for the Mexican Sombrero Lid, but add a snake to the outside edge.

STEP 2. For the flowers, make a black-and-white stacked loaf of clay, running each color through the pasta machine at setting four. Cut into ⅛"-thick slices. Cut a large, yellow flower using the canapé cutter and a button using the Kemper circle cutter. Make a striped loaf using the tomato red and the white clay, cut a small flower using the Kemper flower cutter and a large flower using the canapé cutter. Make button centers for each out of black clay.

STEP 3. Cut leaves out of the leaf green clay with the leaf-shaped canapé cutter; press veins in the leaves with the pro tool. Arrange in a pleasing manner on the lid and smooth any air bubbles and fingerprints with your finger. Bake on baking parchment or rag bond paper at the manufacturer's baking temperature for one hour; then allow to cool in oven before removing it.

GILDED ANTIQUE FRAME

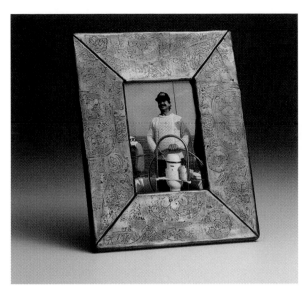

Skill level: Intermediate

MATERIALS

- Cernit, FIMO, or PROMAT (used in project photographed): 6 ounces white (or light color)
- Several good-quality carbon-based photocopies of clipart. Dover's clipart booklets are a good source. I used *Old-Fashioned Floral Illustrations* (booklet number 0-486-26291-X) by Carol Belanger Grafton for this project.
- Food processor (optional)
- Pasta machine
- D&CC (Decorator & Craft Corporation) papier-mâché 3 x 5-inch frame: Number 28-4042
- Tissue slicer
- X-ACTO knife
- Loctite liquid super glue or Sobo glue
- Small icing spatula or palette knife
- Scissors to cut photocopies
- Brayer or rolling pin (A 2-inch piece of plastic piping will also work).
- Baking parchment or rag bond paper
- Oven
- 1-inch soft flat paintbrush
- Delta Ceramcoat acrylic paint: Burnt umber #2025
- Old clean terry-cloth rag
- Rub 'n Buff: Grecian gold #7637IL (This goes a long way and covers well!)

STEP 1. Make several photocopies of your favorite florals. (Old-fashioned ones really make this frame look authentic!) The copies must be carbon-based, not inkjet. Condition the clay, using a food processor, if needed. Roll the clay through the pasta machine on setting three (or four) to $1/16$ inch thickness. Roll two long thin strips and apply them to the long ends of the frame. The strips should be long enough and wide enough to cover these sides, with enough clay to wrap around both the inside and outside frame edges when cut.

STEP 2. Cut with your tissue slicer, allowing an extra $1/8$ inch for overhang wrap. Fold clay over all edges to be sure that it fits. You should have at least a $1/4$-inch overlap on all sides of the strip. Remove the clay.

STEP 3. Apply a liberal amount of Loctite liquid super glue or Sobo glue on one long side of the frame. Using a small icing

spatula or palette knife, thinly spread the glue to cover the one side. Immediately, smooth one of the clay strips onto frame, beginning at the outside edge, making sure that extra ¼ inch is centered top to bottom and left to right, pressing out any air bubbles as you go. Continue down the second side of the frame, using same process. Gently lay the clay strips for the top of the frame over the side strips. Repeat the measuring, cutting, and gluing processes for both the top and the bottom of frame. Be sure to bevel the edges with your tissue

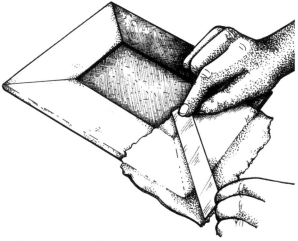

slicer where the top and bottom meet the left and right sides. This makes the frame look professionally done. Wrap and press the remaining ¼ inch over around the edges of the frame; then cut the slot in the top of the frame, so you can slide your pictures in.

STEP 4. Cut photocopies as close to actual printed borders as possible. Lay them printed side down onto the frame in a pleasing arrangement. This step is critical! Do not allow the photocopies to shift or drag on the surface of the clay.

Because the clay liquifies the carbon ink instantly, any shifting will smear the ink and ruin the impression. Remember: If you are using letters, make sure they are printed backward on the photocopy, or the resulting letters will be backward on your frame!

STEP 5. Press the photocopies firmly into the surface of the clay with your fingers. Burnish any air bubbles trapped underneath toward the edge of the paper. Once the copies are well adhered to the frame, carefully roll them flat with a brayer or rolling pin. Let the copies remain on the surface for no longer than ten to fifteen minutes, or the paper will actually pull some of the surface layer of clay off. (Hint: Don't be too concerned if a little chipping occurs—this only makes the frame look more antique!)

STEP 6. Carefully lift one edge of the paper with your X-ACTO knife and peel. If small strands of ink come up with the copy, cut these as soon as you begin lifting with your X-ACTO knife or spatula. (Strands of liquified ink are usually not a problem if you allow the copies to remain on the surface only for up to fifteen minutes.)

STEP 7. Once the entire surface is peeled, let it sit for a moment to allow the ink to settle; then bake it in the oven on a sheet of baking parchment or rag bond paper at the manufacturer's baking temperature for

forty minutes. Allow the frame to cool in the oven before removing. Once cooled, apply a layer of burnt umber Ceramcoat acrylic paint to the surface, using a soft flat paint brush.

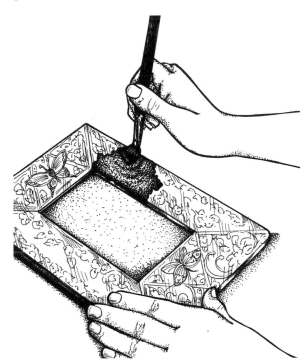

STEP 8. Immediately dab with clean terry-cloth rag. It is important not to rub, because the paint needs to be fairly heavy. It also helps to do one side at a time

because the acrylic paint dries quickly. The dabbing motion will push the paint into the depressions made by the photocopies, giving the frame an antique look. Allow the paint to dry completely.

STEP 9. Add a layer of grecian gold Rub 'n Buff, using a tiny amount on your fingertips and a light feathery touch to apply it. Be careful not to rub too hard, or it will be pressed into the impressions. Once dried, buff the frame with a soft clean cloth. For a more finished look, paint the back and the inside of the photo area; then gild with the Rub 'n Buff.

SPRINGTIME BIRDHOUSE ORNAMENT

Skill level: Intermediate

MATERIALS

- Cernit, Friendly Clay, FIMO, or PROMAT are recommended. Cernit was used in project photographed in the following colors:

    Glamour yellow; Mint no. 1;
    Light green no. 1; Pink no. 1
    Green no. 1; Glamour brown
    Blue-gray no. 1; Lilac no. 1
    Glamour blue

- Food processor (optional)
- Embossing plate (pebble finish) by Enjoyment Products Company
- Pasta machine
- D&CC (Decorator & Craft Corporation) papier-mâché birdhouse: Number 28-0131
- X-ACTO knife
- Loctite liquid super glue
- Small icing spatula or palette knife
- Oven
- Kemper tools/pattern cutters: Flower cutter pcf5, heart cutter pch5, teardrop cutter pct4, teardrop cutter pct3, smallest forget-me-not cutter, pro tool
- Old disassembled ballpoint pen
- Two black 4-millimeter round beads without holes or two large seed beads

STEP 1. Condition all clays, using the food processor, if needed. Roll all clay colors through the pasta machine on setting three to 1/16 inch thickness, except one-half of the lilac. Lay the glamour yellow clay on top of the embossing plate and roll through the pasta machine on setting two.

STEP 2.. Peel the clay from the plate and lay the clay pattern-side up on top of the roof of the house. The clay should be at least 1/8 inch larger than the size of the roof. Once you're satisfied with the placement, run your finger over the clay along the roofline. This will create a indentation in the clay for you to follow when cutting.

STEP 3. Cut downward into the clay with your X-ACTO knife, making a 1/8-inch allowance on all sides for wrapping under the overhang. Remove the clay.

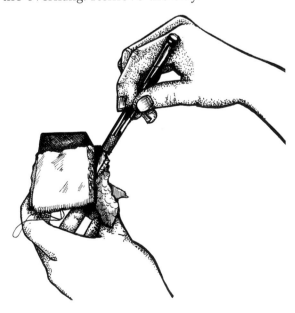

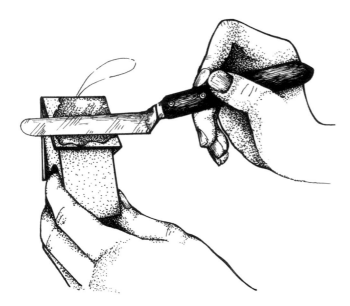

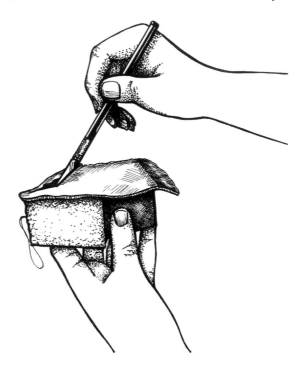

STEP 5. Cut a rectangle out of the mint clay approximately the same size as the front of the birdhouse. Lay the clay rectangle on the front of the house, overlapping by about ¼ inch on all sides. Press the clay

STEP 4. Apply a liberal amount of Loctite liquid super glue to one side of the roof; then thinly spread it over that side using a spatula or a palette knife. Immediately press the clay onto the glued side, beginning at the outside edge and pressing out any air bubbles as you go. Continue down the second side of roof using the same process. Trim any excess clay with your X-ACTO knife. Bake in the oven on a sheet of baking parchment or rag bond paper at the manufacturer's baking temperature, about thirty minutes. Let cool in the oven before removing.

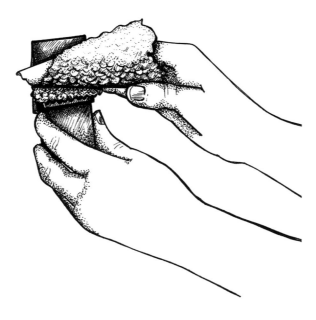

around the outside edges of the birdhouse front, including the roofline. This will create an indentation in the clay for you to follow when cutting. Cut down through the clay with your X-ACTO knife, following the indentations. (Don't worry if it's not exact; the clay can be stretched if it's cut as much as ⅛ inch too short or it can be trimmed if it's cut too large.) Remove the clay. Apply a thin, even layer of Loctite liquid super glue as you did for the roof, slide the peak of the clay pattern you just cut under the peak of the roof on the front of house, and carefully press the clay over the glue, smoothing out air bubbles as you go. Cut a hole for the door using your X-ACTO knife. (Hint: Lightly press inward over the hole with your finger to indent the hole around the edges, so you will know where to cut.) Repeat the same process for the back and sides, smoothing any rough edges as you go with your fingertips, until the entire house is covered.

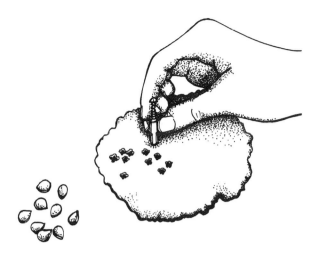

STEP 6. Cut thirteen light green leaves, twenty-two pink flowers, and twenty-four glamour yellow flowers using the Kemper flower cutter, and set aside. Roll three thin snakes with the light pink clay for house trim. Adhere to the right front, right and left rear, and bottom of the house. Be sure to press firmly enough to adhere the pink clay trim to the mint clay on the house. Cut four small light green rectangles for grass, slice into the top half of the rectangle to make the blades, and adhere the bottom, uncut part to the bottom of the house. Pull the blades of grass apart with your finger or X-ACTO knife. Place the twenty-four glamour yellow flowers on top of the grass, using the pro tool to pierce the center of each flower and press it firmly into the grass.

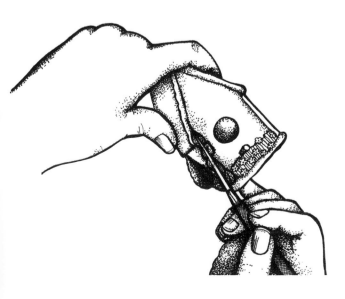

STEP 7. Press the leaves onto the house in a random trailing pattern. Press a vertical line in the center of each leaf with the pro tool. Press each pink flower into place by "stabbing" the center with the pro tool, placing the flower onto the house, and pressing lightly with your fingertip to adhere it. Be sure to burnish out any fingerprints you may have left.

STEP 8. Roll two grape-sized balls of light green clay (one slightly larger than the other) into cone shapes for the two ornamental trees at the left side of the house. Adhere, and press the pro tool into each several times for texture. Make a smaller tree for the rear of house. Roll two green balls of clay for the ornamental tree on the right rear side of the house and use the above method to texture it. Press a small glamour brown clay log under it for the trunk.

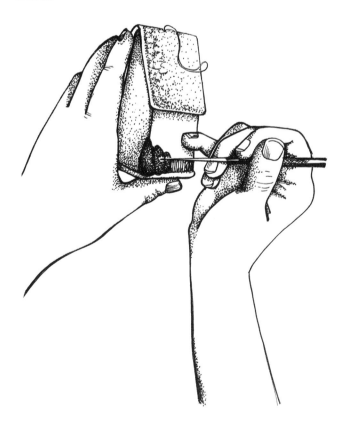

STEP 9. Roll four thin snakes with the green clay, each about 1 inch long and thinner at the top; adhere to the back of the

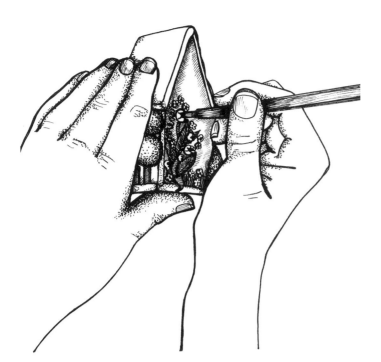

Roll a snake with the glamour yellow clay, about 5 inches long by ⅛ inch in diameter, for the eaves trim in the back of the house, and indent several small hearts into the clay. (Do not cut all the way through the clay, these are just little "halfway through" presses. Also be sure not to depress the plunger of the pattern cutter, or you'll leave a "hole" indentation in each heart!)

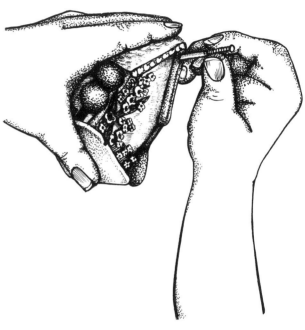

house for the trailing purple flower plant. Press the pro tool lengthwise down the center of each and press leaves forward a bit. Attach thirteen small blue-gray flowers as you did in steps five and six. Make the seven larger flowers by cupping the cut out forget-me-not flower around the end of an old ink pen or a small round brush handle. Press the cupped flowers onto the house. Roll a small snake, about 1 inch long by ⅜ inch in diameter, and attach it to the door for trim. Press three pink hearts onto it and one heart into front peak of the house.

STEP 11. The bird is simple to do! Using the blue-gray clay, roll two grape-sized balls. Shape the bird's head into the shape of a Hershey's kiss and press it onto the body. Cut wings from the rolled out clay using the Kemper teardrop cutter; press details into the wings using the pro tool. Press a tiny cone-shaped yellow beak onto the face. Press two nostrils into the beak and tiny feathers into the chest using the tip of the pro tool. Press eyes into head using an old disassembled ball point pen barrel and two black round beads. Press the barrel into some leftover clay several times to make it sticky and press the tip onto the bead to pick it up. Press the bird where you want him (on roof, on perch, for example) and carefully remove him. Add a dab of Loctite liquid super glue to that spot and press the bird onto it. Bake the birdhouse in the oven on a sheet of baking parchment or rag bond paper at the manufacturer's baking temperature, for thirty-five to forty minutes. Allow it to cool in the oven before removing.

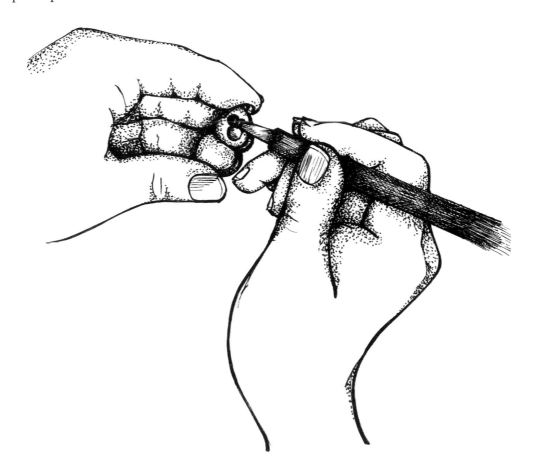

Good Morning, Glory! Garden Soap Dish

Skill level: Intermediate

MATERIALS

- Cernit, Friendly Clay, FIMO, or PROMAT are recommended. Friendly Clay was used in project photographed in the following amounts and colors:

  1/2 ounce orange

  1/4 ounce black

  2 ounces white

  1/2 ounce yellow

  1/4 ounce light blue pearl

  1 ounce translucent

- Food processor (optional)
- Pasta machine
- Typing paper
- Scissors
- Kemper tools/pattern cutters: Pro tool, flower cutter pc5f
- X-ACTO knife
- AMACO Friendly Cutters (leaf shapes)
- Small soft round brush
- Medium brown powdered eye shadow
- Ten-petal floral canapé cutter (or see directions for pattern)
- Old clean terry-cloth rag
- Light blue powdered eye shadow
- Baking parchment or rag bond paper
- Oven

STEP 1. Condition all clays, using a food processor, if needed. All colors in this project are custom-mixed, except those used for the lady bugs. Set aside two (6 millimeter) balls of orange for their bodies and eight black (3 millimeter) flattened balls for their spots and two for their heads. Mix the rest of the orange with all of the white and 1/4 ounce of the yellow to create a medium peach color. Roll a slab of mixed peach clay, about 5½ inches long by 3½ inches wide, through the pasta machine on setting one.

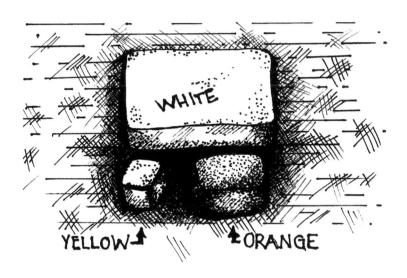

STEP 2. Double the clay thickness by folding it in half.

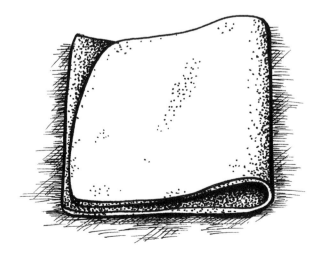

STEP 3. Trace the oval pattern provided onto a piece of typing paper. Cut carefully along the edges with scissors and place the pattern on top of the clay slab. Press the paper lightly to the surface of the clay to adhere it.

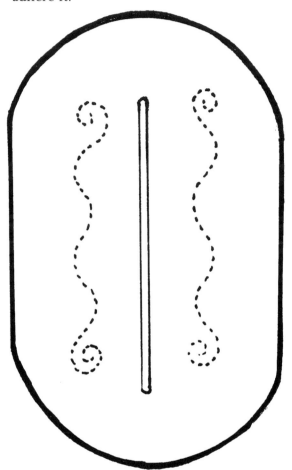

Soap Dish Pattern

STEP 4. Trace around the edge with the pro tool and remove the pattern. Use the

X-ACTO knife to cut along the edge of the pattern through the clay. When finished, remove the paper and smooth the surface of the clay with your fingertip.

STEP 5. Roll the leftover peach clay into a snake, about 16 inches long by ¼ inch in diameter. Beginning at the center back, press the snake firmly around the top outside edge of the soap dish bottom.

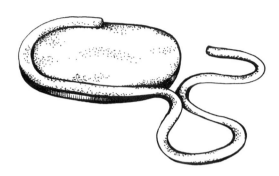

STEP 6. Press a small snake, about 3½ inches long by ¹⁄₁₆ inch in diameter, lengthwise onto the center of the soap dish.

STEP 7. Make a wave design on either side of the soap dish bottom with the pro tool; then press the Kemper flower cutter into the clay four times at the center of each wave.

STEP 8. Roll the yellow through the pasta machine on setting three. Cut three tiny yellow flowers out and set them aside. Mix a dab of black into the remaining yellow to create a medium olive green. Roll the olive green through the pasta machine at setting three. Cut four leaves, two large and two small, using the AMACO Friendly Cutters.

STEP 9. Use the pro tool to press veins into each leaf and arrange leaves over the back edge of the soap dish (see color photo at beginning of project). With a soft brush, carefully dab the medium brown powdered eye shadow onto the center of each leaf.

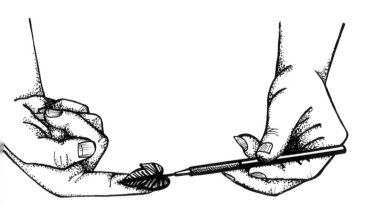

STEP 10. Set aside most of the light blue clay for later use, but mix a tiny pinch (about the size of a pea) with all of the translucent to achieve a very light blue. Roll the translucent/blue clay mixture through the pasta machine at setting three and cut three flowers with the ten-petal floral canapé cutter. Press the side of the pro tool into the large flowers radiating from the center; then press half a line in between. This gives the morning glories a more natural, ruffled look.

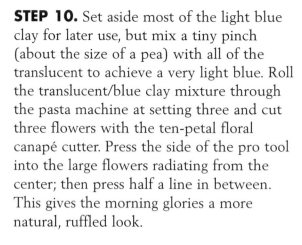
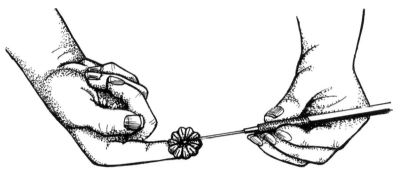

STEP 11. Using the handle end of the paintbrush to press into the center of the flower, gently twist, and cup the clay as you work the flower into a cup shape. Press each flower into place while the brush end is still in place. This will prevent any fingerprints from getting onto the clay.

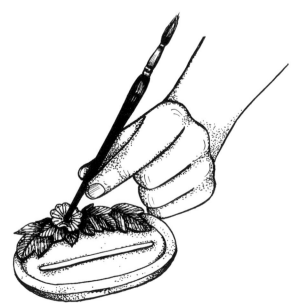

STEP 12. Remove all traces of the brown powdered eye shadow from the soft brush using soap and water; dry by stroking gently on a clean terry-cloth rag. Carefully dab the light blue powdered eye shadow into the center of each flower, making sure you don't streak the powder by stroking it on. Get the three tiny flowers you set aside in step 8, pierce with the pro tool, and gently press into the center of each morning glory with the handle end of the brush.

STEP 13. Cut nine small flowers from the leftover translucent/blue clay mixture using the Kemper flower cutter. Roll the original light blue clay through pasta machine on setting three; then cut twelve light blue flowers, pierce a center hole in each with the pro tool, and place randomly around the larger flowers and leaves.

STEP 14. Take the orange clay that you reserved in step one. Roll two tiny balls out of the clay for the ladybug bodies. Press the pro tool lengthwise into the center of each to make a wing line. Press four tiny black spots on each side of the center line. Roll a black ball of clay for the head and attach it to the body. Roll three tiny thin snakes of black clay, each about ½ inch long, and drape them over the edge of the soap dish to make the legs.

STEP 15. Press one of the ladybug bodies onto the legs and press the other ladybug onto the leaf, to the left of the central large flower. Bake in the oven on a sheet of baking parchment or rag bond paper at the manufacturer's baking temperature for one hour. Let cool in the oven before removing.

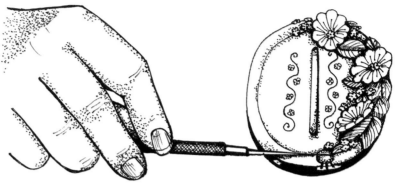

TIP: To keep the soap residue from building on the surface of the soap dish, carefully wash with a soft cloth, dish detergent and warm water. If there is residue in the nooks and crannies, take an old soft toothbrush and carefully scrub the crevices, rinse, and dry. If you want the look without the mess, try making a faux bar of soap out of clay! (What a surprise it will be to your guests when they try to lather up!)

CHRISTMAS PACKAGE FRAME

Skill level: Intermediate

MATERIALS

- PROMAT: 4 ounces red; 2 ounces green; 1 ounce white
- Super Sculpey: 4 ounces
- Food processor (optional)
- Pasta machine
- D&CC (Decorator & Craft Corporation) papier-mâché oval frame: Number 28-4041
- X-ACTO knife with a new blade
- Typing paper
- Small icing spatula or palette knife
- Loctite liquid super glue
- Rough sandpaper (new) or texture tool
- Baking parchment or rag bond paper
- Oven
- Delta Ceramcoat acrylic paint: Red, green
- Flat paintbrush
- Rub 'n Buff: Grecian gold #7637IL
- Embossing plate
- Kemper tools/pattern cutters: Pro tool, star cutter pcs
- FISKARS Paper Edgers scissors
- Rags

STEP 1. Condition the clay, using a food processor, if needed. Roll the red clay through the pasta machine on setting one, turn, and roll through on setting two. The clay should be a rough rectangle, as wide as the roller blades. Return the flattened clay to the pasta machine and carefully roll it through on setting three. The clay sheet should be large enough to cover the frame, but you can stretch it manually if it's not: Take both ends on one side and pull evenly, turn, and do the same on the other side. (Do this step slowly and carefully; if you stretch the clay too far too fast, it will break, and you will have to start over.) Once the clay is large enough to fit and overlap all edges by at least ½ inch, cut to within ¼-inch overlap with your

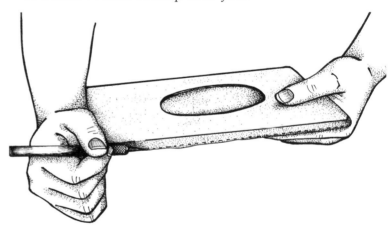

X-ACTO knife, making sure that the edges are covered with clay. If you happen to come up short on an edge, don't worry: You can size and glue strips of clay to even things out later.

STEP 2. Carefully remove the clay from the frame and set it (face up) close by on a clean sheet of typing paper. Using a small icing spatula or palette knife, spread a thin even layer of Loctite liquid super glue around the frame, beginning at the top edge and continuing halfway down the frame to the middle. Immediately, position the clay you cut for the frame over the glued area, beginning at the top edge. Press any air bubbles out as you place the clay over the glue. Continue this process until the frame is evenly covered. Repeat process for edges, cut the slot for the picture, and trim any remaining clay from the edges.

STEP 3. Press into the clay with the rough sandpaper or roll the texture tool over it until entire frame is evenly textured, including the edges.

Note: If you have difficulty handling the frame without obliterating the texture (or if you simply want to avoid ruining your hard work by overhandling it), bake it now on a sheet of baking parchment or rag bond paper at the manufacturer's baking temperature for one hour; then move on to step four and glue the remaining pieces to the baked clay.

If you opt not to bake at this point, jump to step twelve. You'll save a little glue by adhering the remaining pieces to the raw clay.

STEP 4. Roll a large sheet of green clay about 6 inches long by 6 inches wide, through the pasta machine on setting three. Cut the sheet in half, to the size of the embossing plate, and roll the clay and plate through pasta machine on setting two.

STEP 5. Cut two strips of green clay, each about 3½ inches long by ⅝ inch wide, for the flat, or "backing," ribbon. Attach both to the frame, running the ribbon sheet over the top edge and into the oval open edge of the frame.

STEP 6. Cut two more slightly wider strips, each measuring 4 inches long and loop in half, with the top of the loop facing the frame opening. Cut, loop, and press two more loops for the top, each 2 inches long; then press on top of the last loops, in the

same direction. Press the pro tool in the open edge of each loop three times to create the illusion of folds.

STEP 7. For the left and right sides of the ribbon, repeat the above steps, but use two strips each about 2½ inches long by 1¼ inches wide for the flat, or backing, ribbon and four strips each about 2½ inches long by 1¼ inches wide for the loops.

STEP 8. Make a FISKARS Paper Edgers trim around the oval opening of the frame by rolling a sheet of white clay through the pasta machine on setting four, cutting four strips (each measuring about 3 inches long),

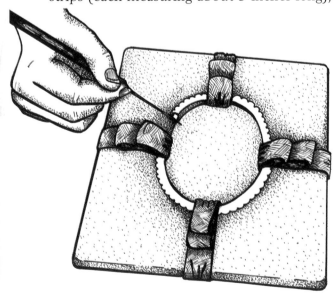

and pressing to the edge of the opening with the pro tool.

STEP 9. To make Santa's arms, roll two snakes out of red clay, each about 1¼ inches long. Attach the arms side-by-side at the top right edge of the frame. Make two balls from the green clay, press them below the arms for the hands, and cut a slit in each for the thumbs, using the X-ACTO knife.

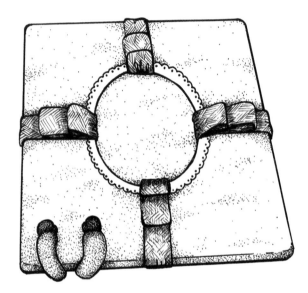

STEP 10. Roll two tiny thin snakes for the trim on Santa's coat out of the white clay and press them above the mittens, cutting away any excess clay with your X-ACTO knife. Carefully texture Santa's arms with the tip of the pro tool.

STEP 11. To make Santa's face and hat, roll a grape-sized ball of flesh clay and press it between the arms at the top of the frame. Roll a sheet of white clay through the pasta machine on setting three for the beard and trace the pattern provided at right on a separate sheet of typing paper. Lay your pattern on the top of the white sheet of clay and cut it out with the X-ACTO knife. For the moustache, roll a long snake with the white

clay. Taper the ends and press it above the beard. Add a tiny ball of flesh clay for the nose. Make a cone-shaped hat, fold it over onto itself, and attach to the top of Santa's head. Add a small white pom-pom to the top of the hat and a white snake along the bottom for trim. Carefully texture the red part of Santa's hat with the tip of the pro tool.

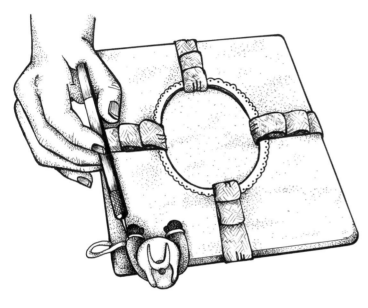

STEP 12. If you opted not to bake the frame after texturing it as described in step three, cut eleven large stars from the white clay using the larger Kemper star pattern cutters and press in a pleasing arrangement onto the frame. You may wish to texture some of the larger stars using an embossing plate, or small-grid plastic canvas. Cut four smaller stars and press where shown. If you opted to bake the frame first, attach the stars and Santa with Loctite liquid super glue.

STEP 13. On a sheet of rag bond or baking parchment bake the frame at the manufacturer's baking temperature for one hour; then allow to cool in oven before removing. Paint the oval and back of the frame using red and green Ceramcoat acrylic paint and gild the ribbons and stars using grecian gold Rub 'n Buff.

RECYCLED SANTA LIGHTBULB ORNAMENT

Skill level: Intermediate

MATERIALS

- Cernit, Friendly Clay, FIMO, or PROMAT are recommended. Cernit was used in project photographed in the following amounts and colors:

    1 ounce white; ½ ounce red;

    ¼ ounce flesh; ⅛ ounce green

- Food processor (optional)
- Pasta machine
- X-ACTO knife
- Old burned-out night-light bulb or large Christmas tree light bulb
- Kemper tools/pattern cutters: Round cutter pc2r, heart cutter pcbh, star cutter pc3st, pro tool
- Old disassembled ball point pen
- Two black 3-millimeter solid eye beads or two black seed beads
- Pliers
- 6 inches of plastic-coated phone wire (red and green) or bare copper or 16-gauge floral wire
- Loctite liquid super glue
- Texture tool or old toothbrush
- Baking parchment or rag bond paper
- Oven

STEP 1. Condition all clays, using a food processor, if needed. Roll the white clay through the pasta machine on setting three. Using your X-ACTO knife, cut the white clay into a rough rectangle, about 4 inches long by 3 inches wide.

STEP 2. Begin at the top edge of the glass part of the bulb and slightly stretch the clay as you wrap the bulb tightly.

STEP 3. Continue stretching and wrapping the clay all the way around the bulb until you overlap the first line of clay.

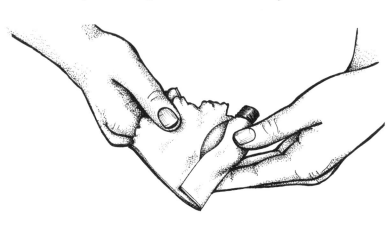

STEP 4. Trim the excess clay using your X-ACTO knife.

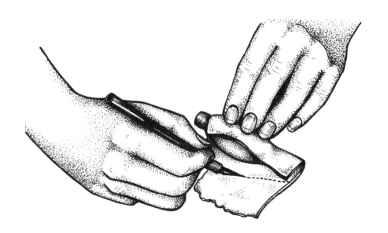

STEP 5. Smooth the clay by rolling in the palms of your hands; the slight overlap of clay will disappear. Press out or slice into with your X-ACTO knife any air bubbles trapped under the surface, so that Santa's beard is smooth and bubble free.

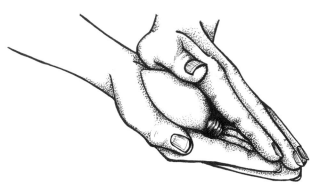

STEP 6. Roll the red clay through the pasta machine on setting three; then cut a rectangle, about 2 inches long by 1 inch wide, using your X-ACTO knife. Wrap this around the screw end of the bulb and smooth any trapped bubbles before sealing the clay to the top. Follow the line of the bulb end, bringing the clay to a slightly rounded tip.

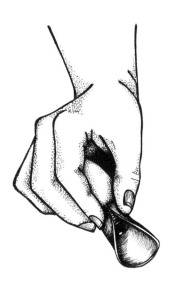

STEP 7. Roll a snake with the white clay, about 3 inches long by 1/8 inch in diameter, point both ends, and set aside. This will be Santa's moustache. Roll another white snake, about 4 inches long and 1/4 inch in diameter, and press it where the hat meets the top of Santa's head. Meet the two ends in the back and smooth the edges together with your X-ACTO knife to hide the seam and seal the gap.

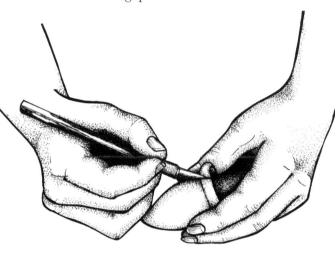

STEP 8. Roll the flesh clay through the pasta machine on setting three and cut a heart-shaped face using the Kemper heart cutter.

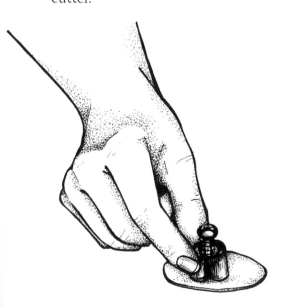

STEP 9. Press the face just below the hat brim.

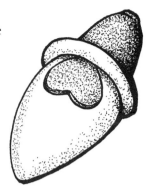

STEP 10. Cut the two cheeks from red clay using the Kemper round cutter, and press at the two rounded lobes of the heart

STEP 11. Press the moustache you set aside in step seven onto the lower third of the face with the pro tool. Roll a small pink ball for the nose and place it above the moustache. Press the pro tool into the vertical center of the moustache to make a dividing line.

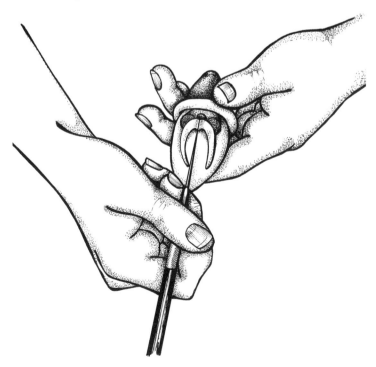

STEP 12. Using an old disassembled ball point pen barrel, press the two black solid eye beads into the face between and slightly above the cheeks.

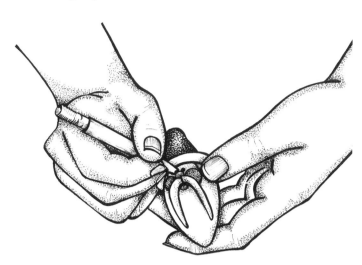

STEP 14. Roll a white pom-pom about the size of a small grape. Press it to the tip of Santa's hat.

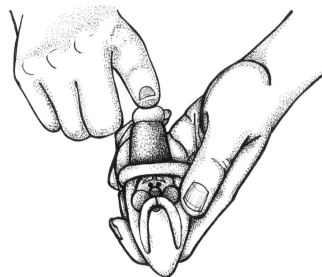

STEP 13. Roll a tiny double-pointed white snake for the eyebrows. Cut it in half and press the two halves in place using the pro tool.

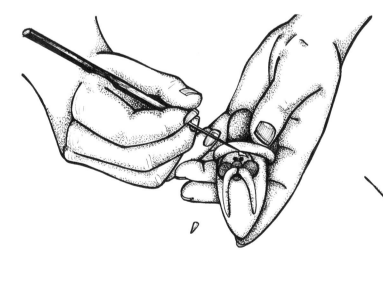

STEP 15. Using your pliers, twist the wire together to form a braid, loop it, and twist the open ends closed; this loop will be the hanger. Poke a hole in the top of the pom-pom with the pro tool to accommodate the wire, put some Loctite liquid super glue on the end of the twisted wire, and press the wire into the hole. Allow the glue to dry and smooth the clay up over the hole to strengthen the bond.

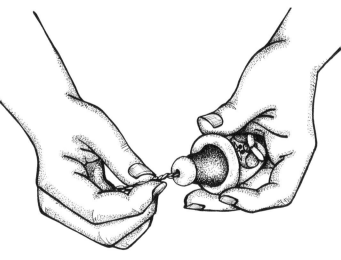

STEP 16. Using a texture tool or an old toothbrush, texture Santa's beard and moustache.

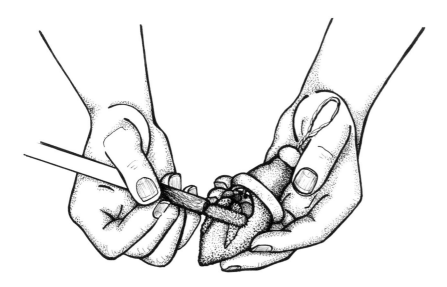

STEP 17. Cut seven green stars with the Kemper star cutter and position them around the top of the brim of Santa's hat using the pro tool. Bake in the oven on a sheet of baking parchment or rag bond paper at the manufacturer's baking temperature for forty-five minutes. Let it cool in the oven before removing.

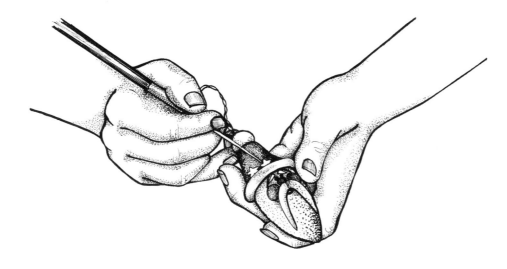

CHRISTMAS TREE BOX

Skill level: Advanced

MATERIALS

- Cernit (opaque white), FIMO (green), and PROMAT (red) were used in the project photographed because of their specific colors. If you are not as set on these exact color results, use any of the three clays in the following amounts and colors:

    4 ounces white; 6 ounces red;
    6 ounces green; 1 ounce gold

- Food processor (optional)
- Pasta machine
- X-ACTO Knife
- D&CC (Decorator & Craft Corporation) papier-mâché Christmas tree box: Number 28-0018
- Small icing spatula or palette knife
- Loctite liquid super glue
- Kemper tools/pattern cutters: Large star cutter pc3st, small star cutter pcbst, pro tool
- Baking parchment or rag bond paper
- Oven
- FISKARS Paper Edgers scissors: Purple handle
- Delta Ceramcoat acrylic paint: Jubilee green #2421, bright red #2503
- 1-inch flat soft brush
- Matte sealer or varnish (optional)

STEP 1. Condition all clays, using a food processor, if needed. Roll all clay colors through the pasta machine on setting four to $1/16$ inch thickness. To make a striped loaf, run 2 ounces of red clay and 2 ounces of white clay through pasta machine at setting one. Stack the red on top of the white. Press clays tightly together, making sure that there are no air bubbles trapped underneath. Cut any excess clay and square the edges up using your X-ACTO knife.

STEP 2. Roll the striped loaf through the pasta machine on setting three, to thin it out and to help the two clays adhere together. Cut the cane in half, stack, and adhere, making sure there are no air bubbles between. Repeat the cutting-and-stacking method until you have a striped loaf with fifteen to twenty-four stripes. Let the loaf rest for a few hours, or place it in the refrigerator for thirty minutes to cool. This will allow for more precision cutting.

STEP 3. Using the top of the tree box as a template, press the inside edge into the green clay slab to imprint an outline. Trace around this outline with your X-ACTO knife.

STEP 4. Using a spatula, spread a liberal amount of Loctite liquid super glue in a thin layer over the papier-mâché box top. Press the clay tree cutout shape onto the top of the box lid, making sure that no air bubbles are trapped beneath. Burnish the clay with your fingertips to remove any fingerprints or gouges.

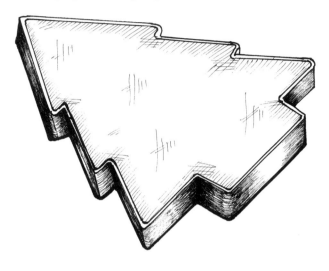

STEP 5. Roll several red pea-sized clay balls into half-round "candies," similar in shape to M&M's, and press them onto the tree.

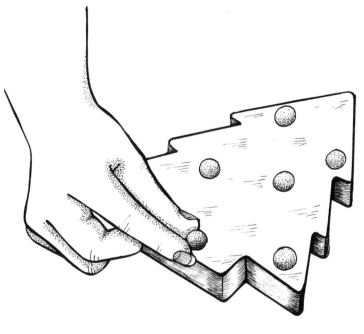

STEP 6. Cut the striped cane into nine thin leaves, about 1/16 inch thick.

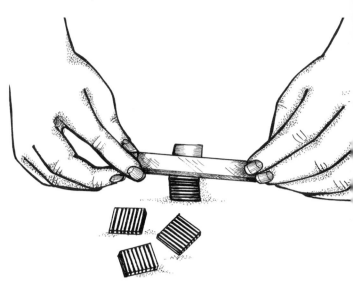

STEP 7. Press them randomly onto the surface of the lid. Set one at the bottom right corner of the tree. Cut one striped slice in half against the stripes, and place half on the top left-hand bough of the tree, and the other on the bottom left-hand tree bough. Cut any overlapping edges with your X-ACTO knife.

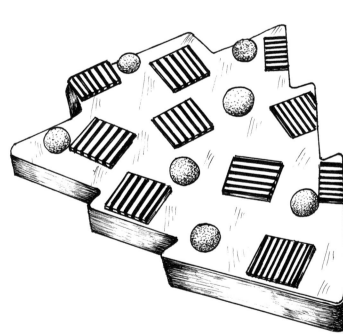

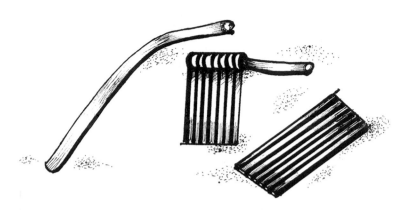

STEP 10. Cut two thin red strips, each 10 inches long by ¾ inch wide, for the sides of the box. Using a small icing spatula or palette knife, spread Loctite liquid super glue on one section (bough) at a time, and press clay on to cover each section. Continue around entire edge of box top.

STEP 8. Roll four snakes out of the white clay, each about 1¼ inches long by ⅛ inch in diameter. Wrap a thin layer of the striped cane around each, trim, and form into a candy cane shape.

STEP 9. Press the candy canes onto the tree. Roll a rope from the gold clay, about 22 inches long by ¹⁄₁₆ inch in diameter, and crisscross down the tree. Use Kemper star cutters, cut out twenty to twenty-two large gold stars and sixteen to twenty small gold stars. Press in a random pattern atop the gold rope. Bake in the oven on a sheet of baking parchment or rag bond paper at 250 degrees for one hour. Allow to cool in the oven before removing.

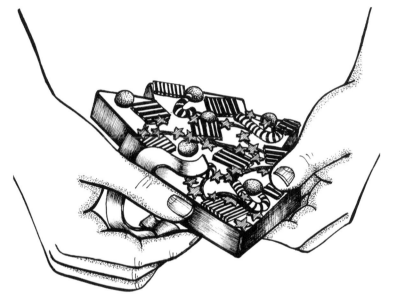

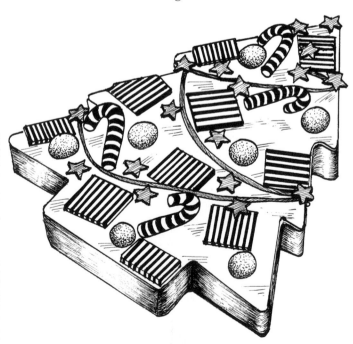

STEP 11. Using the FISKARS Paper Edgers scissors, cut two white trim pieces, each 10 inches long, and trim the edges so that the lace is about ¼ inch wide. Mount just above the edge of the box lid. Pierce holes into the center top of every rounded peak with the pro tool. Smooth any air bubbles and burnish any fingerprints or gouges as you go. Bake again at 250 degrees for one hour and allow to cool in the oven before removing.

STEP 12. Bottom of box: Follow the directions in steps three and four to cut a sheet of red clay to cover the bottom of the box. Roll remaining red clay through the pasta machine on setting four. Cut two red clay strips, each 10 inches long by 3 inches wide, for the sides of box bottom. The clay is cut short widthwise so the lid will fit, so start applying the clay about ½ inch below the top edge.

STEP 13. Beginning at the side of the box (at the "tip" of the tree), spread a thin layer of Loctite liquid super glue with a small icing spatula or palette knife, one section at a time. Cover the sides with a red clay strip.

Be sure to butt the bottom of the edge to the clay covering the bottom of the box. Continue to spread each section completely with glue and to stretch the clay slightly taut when applying the clay. This evens out the clay and makes it easier to press on. Continue gluing and

pressing until all sides of the tree box bottom are covered with red. Press any air bubbles out as you work.

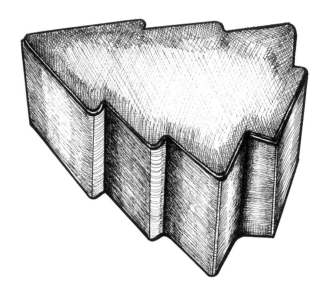

STEP 14. Cut another white strip for the bottom trim, using the FISKARS Paper Edgers scissors. Press holes as before and press the pro tool into the corners of the tree box to adhere the trim.

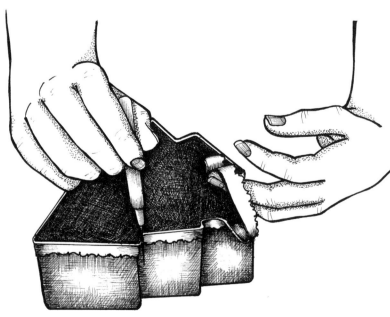

STEP 15. Roll two clay snakes, one green and one white, each measuring 6 inches long by ⅛ inch in diameter. Twist them together and roll until they mesh.

STEP 16. Press the green-and-white roll along the top edge of the box bottom, pressing the indentations in with the pro tool. Bake in the oven on a sheet of baking parchment or rag bond paper at the manufacturer's baking temperature for one hour; then allow it to cool in the oven before removing.

STEP 17. With a flat soft brush, paint the outside of the top edge and the inside of the box bottom green and the inside of the top red or green. Use three to four coats, brushing in opposite directions for each coat, allowing each coat to dry in between. If desired, coat the inside and outside painted areas with a matte sealer or varnish.

IDEAS

Rather than painting the inside of the box, you can cover it with fabric. Use it for chocolates, homemade cookies, dried fruits, nuts, Christmas potpourri, or treasured cards. Maybe you'd like to give mini candy canes to someone special, make faux candy cane ornaments to adorn the tree, or bake Grandma's Old-Fashioned "No Cal" Cookies (see page 44)—and place them inside!

RESOURCES

COMPANIES

Accent Import-Export, Inc.
P.O. Box 4361
Walnut Creek, CA 94596
Phone: (510) 827-2889

FIMO and FIMO-related products.

American Art Clay Company (AMACO)
4717 West Sixteenth Street
Indianapolis, IN 46222
Phone: (317) 244-6871 or
1-800-374-1600
Fax: (317) 248-9300

FIMO and Friendly Clay, molds,
Friendly Cutters, Friendly Clay plastic
Goop, Rub 'n Buff, Friendly Clay
Millefiori Canes, FIMO metallic pow-
ders, and polymer clay books.

Clay Factory of Escondido
P.O. Box 460598
Escondido, CA 92046-0598
Phone: 1-800-243-3466
Fax: (619) 741-5436

Sculpey III, PROMAT, Cernit, and
many polymer clay supplies.

Craft King Discount Craft Supply
P.O. Box 90637
Lakeland, FL 33804
Phone: 1-800-769-9494
Fax: (941) 648-2972

Sculpey, PROMAT, Granitex, Cernit,
FIMO, tools, and books.

CraftWoods
2101 Greenspring Drive
Timonium, MD 21093
Phone: (410) 561-9444 or
1-800-468-7070
Fax: (410) 560-0760

Powders, Foredom tools and
accessories, an assortment of wood-
working tools, copper and brass tubing
and wire, and many other items that
may be used on polymer clay.

Decorator and Craft Corporation (D&CC)
428 South Zelta
Wichita, KS 67207-1499
Phone: 1-800-835-3013
Fax: (316) 685-7606

Papier-mâché birdhouses, frames,
boxes, and many other shapes.

Enjoyment Products
225 Dean Street
Providence, RI 02903
Phone: (401) 421-0261
Fax: (401) 831-9828

Metal texture plates, cabochon molds,
jewelry findings.

FISKARS
7811 West Stewart Avenue
Wausau, WI 54401
Phone: 1-800-950-0203 or
(715) 842-2091
Fax: (715) 858-5528

Paper Edgers scissors.

Handcraft Designs, Inc.
63 East Broad Street
Hatfield, PA 19440
Phone: (215) 855-3022

Cernit, books, and related items.

Hot Off the Press, Inc.
1250 N W Third
Canby, OR 97013
Phone: (503) 266-9102
Fax: (503) 266-8749

Polymer clay books, the Klay Gun, and assorted Kemper pattern cutters.

Houston Art and Frame
P.O. Box 27164
2520 Drexel Drive
Houston, TX 77027
Phone: (713) 868-7570

Gold, silver, and copper composition and leafing.

Jerry's Artarama
P.O. Box 1150
New Hyde Park, NY 11040
Phone: 1-800-827-8478
Fax: (516) 328-6752

Polymer clay, tools, supplies, leafing, paints, and many more arts and crafts items.

Kemper Enterprises, Inc.
13595 12th St.
Chino, CA 91710
Phone: (909) 627-6191 or
1-800-388-5367
Fax: (909) 627-4008

Polymer clay tools, books, the Klay Gun, assorted Kemper pattern cutters, and Cernit.

Jaquard Products
Rupert, Gibbon & Spider, Inc.
1147 Healdsburg Avenue
Healdsburg, CA 95448
Phone: (707) 433-9577
Fax: (707) 433-4906

Metallic powders and interference powders.

The Leather Factory
P.O. Box 50429
Dept. 1CT96
Fort Worth, TX 76105
Phone: (817) 496-4414
Fax: (817) 496-9806

Leather-working tools.

Loctite Corporation
1001 Trout Brook Crossing
Rocky Hill, CT 06067
Phone: (203) 571-5100
Fax: (203) 571-5465

Loctite Liquid Super Glue, Quick Tite Super Glue, and Creatively Yours Super Glue.

Munro-Avante
3954 West 12 Mile Road
Berkley, MI 48072
Phone: (810) 544-1590 or
1-800-638-0543
Fax: (810) 544-0357

All popular brands of polymer clay, tools, books, and just about any other craft supply imaginable!

Off the Beaten Path
3837 North Elmwood #1
Kansas City, MO 64117
Phone: (816) 455-6348

Miniature cookie cutters in many shapes.

Polyform Corporation
1901 Estes
Elk Grove Village, IL 60007
Phone: (708) 427-0020
Fax: (708) 427-0426

Sculpey III, Granitex, PROMAT, Polyform, Sculpey, and Super Sculpey.

SAX Arts & Crafts
P.O. Box 51710
New Berlin, WI 53151
Phone: 1-800-323-0388
Fax: (414) 784-1176

Polymer clay, tools, books, art supplies.

Thomas Scientific
99 High Hill Road
I-295 Box 99
Swedesboro, NJ 08085-0099
Phone: 1-800-345-2100

Tissue slicing blades (order part number 6727-C18).

Wee Folk Creations
18476 Natchez Avenue
Prior Lake, MN 55732
Phone: (612) 447-3828
Fax: (612) 447-8816 (24 hours)

A variety of polymer-related products, including clay, books, and tools.

Wilton
2240 West 12th Street
Woodridge, IL 60517
Phone: (708) 963-7100

Plastic cookie cutters.

TRADE ASSOCIATIONS

ACCI (Association of Crafts and Creative Industries, Inc.)
1100-H Brandywine Boulevard
P.O. Box 2188
Zanesville, OH 43702-2188

HIA (Hobby Industries Association)
319 East 54th Street
P.O. Box 348
Elmwood Park, NJ 07407
Phone: (201) 794-1133
Fax: (201) 797-0657

MAGAZINES

CNA (Craft and Needlework Age)
Hobby Publications, Inc.
225 Gordons Corner Plaza,
Box 420
Manalpan, NJ 07726
Phone: (908) 446-4900

Craftrends
3761 Venture Drive
Suite 140
Duluth, GA 30136
Phone: (770) 497-1500
E-mail: Craftrends

PROFESSIONAL ASSOCIATIONS

The National Polymer Clay Guild
Suite 115-345
1350 Beverly Road
McLean, VA 22101
Phone: (202) 895-5212

Society of Craft Designers
P.O Box 2188
Zanesville, OH 43702-2188
Phone: (614) 452-4541
Fax: (614) 452-2552
E-mail:scd@offinger.com

BOOKS

The New Clay (ISBN: 0-9620543-4-8) by Nan Roche, Flower Valley Press, 4806 Camelot St., Rockville, MD 20853.

Creative Clay Jewelry (ISBN: 0-937274-74-7) by Leslie Dierks, Lark Books, 50 College St., Asheville, NC 28801.

Creating with Polymer Clay Designs, Techniques & Projects (ISBN: 0-937374-95-X) by Steven Ford and Leslie Dierks, Lark Books, 50 College St., Asheville, NC 28801.

The Art of Making & Marketing Art Dolls
(ISBN: 0-916809-80-3) by Jack Johnston,
Scott Publications, 30595 Eight Mile Rd.,
Livonia, MI 48152.

Fantastic Figures (ISBN: 0-914881-00-0) by
Suzanna Oroyan, C & T Publishing, P.O.
Box 1456, Lafayette, CA 94549.

Making Original & Portrait Dolls in Cernit
(ISBN: 0-87588-394-X) by Rotraut
Schrott, Hobby House Press Inc., 1
Corporate Drive, Grantsville, MD 21536.

Neato FIMO Menagerie (ISBN: 1-56231-
151-4) by Kris Richards, Hot Off The Press,
1250 N.W. Third, Canby, OR 97013.

*FIMO Animals Two By Two, Noah, The Ark,
and All Those Critters* (ISBN: 1-56321-174-
3) by Kris Richards, Hot Off the Press,
1250 N.W. Third, Canby, OR 97013.

Cutting Up With Clay (ISBN: 1-56321-206-
5) by Kris Richards and Donna Kato,
Hot Off The Press, 1250 N.W. Third,
Canby, OR 97013.

Create With Clay The Sculpey Way (ISBN:
1-56321-250-2) by Kris Richards, Hot Off
The Press, 1250 N.W. Third, Canby, OR
97013.

VIDEOS

Mastering The New Clay, by Tory Hughes,
Gameplan ArtRanch, 2233 McKinley,
Berkeley, CA 94703. This is part of her
series on imitative techniques, bead shapes,
mokume gane, vessels, boxes, pots, and
bowls. For more information, call (510)
549-0093.

Several videos by Maureen Carlson are
available through Wee Folk, 18476 Natchez
Avenue, Prior Lake, MN 55732. Phone:
(612) 447-3828, fax: (612) 447-8816 (24
hours).

ONLINE AND INTERNET SERVICES RELATING TO POLYMER CLAY

ProCrafter's (The Professional Crafter from American Craft Malls)
Web address:
http://www.procrafter.com/procraft

Craftnet Village
David Larson Productions
Web Address: http://www.craftnet.org

A World of Crafts from Cutting Edge Distribution
Web Address:
http://www.craft.com/craft

Creativity Connection from ACCI
Web Address:
http://www.connect2.org/cc

PUBLICATIONS OF INTEREST

Bead & Button Magazine, Conterie Press Inc., 316 Occidental Avenue South, Burke Building Suite 316, Seattle, WA 98104. Subscriptions: 1-800-400-2482, editorial office: (206) 287-0071. This bimonthly publication includes polymer clay designs in almost every issue.

Jewelry Crafts Magazine, Miller Magazines, Inc., 4880 Market Street, Ventura, CA 93003. Phone: (805) 644-3824. This bimonthly publication includes polymer clay designs in almost every issue.

American Craft Magazine (A publication of the American Craft Council), 72 Spring Street, New York, NY 10012-4019. Phone: (212) 274-0630, fax: (212) 274-0650. This bimonthly publication has gorgeous craft work and wonderful articles—very inspirational!

Ornament Magazine, 230 Keystone Way, Vista, CA 92083. Subscriptions: P.O. Box 2349, San Marcos, CA 92079-2349. Phone: (619) 599-0222. This quarterly publication provides wonderful inspiration for the crafter/artisan and features regular articles by well-known polymer clay artists.

Lapidary Journal, Devon Office Center Suite 201, 60 Chestnut Avenue, Devon, PA 19333-1312. Phone: (610) 293-1112. This monthly publication is packed with ideas, inspiration, polymer clay workshops, and good product resources.

INDEX

Acrylic paint on polymer clays, 26
Added finishes, 32–33
American Art Clay Company (AMACO),
  26–27, 30, 89
The Art of Making and Marketing Art Dolls
  (Johnston), 29
Association of Crafts and Creative
  Industries, Inc. (ACCI), 91
Association resources, professional and
  trade, 91

Baking process
  for beads, 29
  for Cernit polymer clay, 5
  for finishes, 26
  for Friendly Clay polymer clay, 11, 13
  glues for, 30–32
  for Granitex polymer clay, 13
  items for baking on, 28–30
  molds and, 28
  in "nest," 29–30
  for PROMAT polymer clay, 28
  rules, general, 28
  safety tips, 15, 32
  for Sculpey III polymer clay, 15, 28
  for Super Sculpey polymer clay, 16
  surface for, 29
Basics (category of Sculpey III colors), 14
Beads, baking process for, 29
Bench grinder, 22
Birdhouse ornament, making, 60–65
Book resources, xi, 29, 91–92
Box, making Christmas tree, 82–87
Brands of polymer clays. *See also*
  Conditioning polymer clays
  Cernit
    baking process for, 5
    color mixing, 39
    colors of, 5
    described, 3–5
    Glamour, 32
    uses of, 5
  color intensity scale for, 17
  conditioning time scale for, 17
  dividing, 3

FIMO
  color mixing, 38–39
  colors of, 5, 11, 32
  date of, 7
  described, 5–7
  Friendly Clay and, similarities to,
    11, 13
  Glamour colors of, 5
  shelf life of, 7
  Stone colors of, 5, 11
  translucent formulas of, 5
  uses for, 5, 7
Friendly Clay, 11, 13, 39
Granitex, 10, 13, 15, 32
intensity scale for, 17
popular, 2
PROMAT
  baking process for, 28
  colors of, 13
  described, 13
Sculpey III
  baking process for, 15, 28
  color mixing, 14, 39
  colors of, 14
  described, 14
  finish of, 32
  Polyform polymer clay and, 15–16, 32
  predictable factors of, 14–15
Sculpey/Polyform, 15–16, 32
Super Sculpey, 16
tensile strength of, 16
varieties of, 2
Brights (category of Sculpey III colors), 14

Carlson, Maureen, 21
Carnival Arts, 33
Cernit polymer clay
  baking process for, 5
  color mixing, 39
  colors of, 5
  described, 3–5
  Glamour, 32
  uses for, 5
Chocolate Sweets for the Dieter project,
  42–43

Christmas ornaments, making
   birdhouse, 60–65
   Santa lightbulb, 77–81
Christmas Package Frame project, 72–76
Christmas Tree Box project, 82–87
Clay Factory of Escondido, 89
Clean-up after working with polymer
   clays, 33–35
Color intensity scale, 17
Color mixing technique, 36–39
Colors
   acrylic paint, 26
   of Cernit polymer clay, 5
   of FIMO polymer clay, 5, 11, 32
   intensity scale for, 17
   intermediary, 38
   makeup, 26
   marbleizing, 36
   mixing, 36-39
   paint, 26
   primary, 36–37
   of PROMAT polymer clay, 13
   of Sculpey III polymer clay, 14
   secondary, 36–38
   shade and, 36
   tertiary, 38
   tinting and, 36
   tone and, 36
Conditioning polymer clays
   FIMO
      with food processor, 8–9
      heat, 11
      with heating pad, 9, 11
      Mix Quick, 7
      oil, 7–8
      with pasta machine, 9
      storage after, 35
      warm water and bag, 11
   Friendly Clay, 13
   large amounts, 39
   PROMAT, 14–15
   Sculpey III, 15
   storage after, 35
   time scale for, 17
Copper, patinas of, 32
Craft King Discount Craft Supply, 89
Crafts (manufacturer), 30

CraftWoods, 89
Creatively Yours glue, 30
Cyanoacrylate ester glue, 30

Darice, Inc., 89
Decorator and Craft Corporation (D&CC),
   89
Delta (manufacturer), 33
Dremel Mototool, 22
Dremel Spray furniture polish, 33

E 6000 glue, 30
Eberhard Faber, 11, 33
Elmer's glue, 30
Enjoyment Products Company, 27
Epoxy glues, 30

Faux candy, making, 42–43
Faux cookies, making, 44–47
Faux techniques, polymer clays for, 5,
   7, 28
FIMO polymer clay
   color mixing, 38–39
   colors of, 5, 11, 32
   conditioning
      with food processor, 8-9
      heat, 11
      with heating pad, 9, 11
      Mix Quick, 7
      oil, 7–8
      with pasta machine, 9
      storage after, 35
      with warm water and bag, 11
   described, 5–7
   Friendly Clay and, similarities to, 11, 13
   Glamour colors of, 5
   shelf life of, 7
   Stone colors of, 5, 11
   translucent formulas of, 5
   uses for, 5, 7
Finishes, 26, 32-33
Fiskars (manufacturer), 89
Fluorescent bulbs, for lighting work
   area, 19
Food processor, for conditioning FIMO,
   8–9
Foredom polisher/buffer, 22

Found objects for texture, 24
Frames, making picture
    Christmas package, 72–76
    gilded antique, 56–59
Friendly Clay polymer clay, 11, 13, 39
Friendly Clay softener, 13
Friendly Plastic Arts glue, 30
Full-color mixing methods, 38–39
Future floor wax, 33

Gilded Antique Frame project, 56–59
Glamour Cernit, 32
Glamour colors of FIMO, 5
Glow-in-the-dark polymer clay, 13
Glues for baking process, 30–32
Good Morning, Glory! Garden Soap Dish
    project, 66–71
GOOP glue, 30
Gooseneck lamp, for lighting work area, 19
Grandma's Old-Fashioned "No-Cal" Sugar
    Cookies project, 44–47
Granitex polymer clay, 10, 13, 15, 32

Handcraft Designs, Inc., 89
Heat conditioning of FIMO, 11
Heating pad, for conditioning FIMO, 9, 11
Hobby Industries Association (HIA), 91
Hot glue, 30
Hot Off the Press, Inc., 90
Houston Art and Frame, 90
Hughes, Tory, 21, 23, 28

Imitative techniques, polymer clays for, 5,
    7, 28
Ink pen, making, 48–51
Intermediary colors, 38
Intermediates (category of Sculpey III
    colors), 14
Internet Ink Pen project, 48–51
Internet resources, 92

Jaquard Products, 90
Jar lids, making, 52–55
Jerry's Artarama, 90
Johnson's paste wax, 33
Johnston, Jack, 29

Kemper Enterprises, Inc., 90
Kemper tools, 20–21
Klay Gun, 20–21
Krylon (manufacturer), 33

Lacquers, 26, 32–33
Leaf cutters, 20
The Leather Factory, 90
Lexan work surface, 18–19
Lids, making jar, 52–55
Lighting of work area, 19
Loctite Corporation, 30–31, 90
Loctite glues, 30–31
Lucite work surface, 18–19

Magazine resources, 91, 93
Makeup on polymer clays, 26
Marbleizing technique, 36
Matte spray coating, 33
Metal cabochon molds, 27
Millefiori technique, polymer clays for, 5, 7
Mix Quick conditioning, 7
Mix Quick Kneading Medium, 7, 13
Molds, making and using, 26–28
Munro-Avante (manufacturer), 90

National Polymer Clay Guild, xi, 91
Natural light, for lighting work area, 19
Needle tool, 20
The New Clay (Roche), xi
Nightglow PROMAT, 13
Nontraditional tools for working with
    polymer clay, 21–22

Off the Beaten Path (manufacturer), 90
Oil conditioning of FIMO, 7–8
Online resources, 92
Ornaments, making
    birdhouse, 60–65
    Santa lightbulb, 77–81

Paint on polymer clays, 26
Pasta machine
    cleaning, 34–35
    for conditioning FIMO, 9
Paste wax, 33

Patina finish, 32
Pattern cutters, 20
Pearls (category of Sculpey III colors), 14
Pen, making, 48–51
Picture frames, making
    antique, 56–59
    Christmas package, 72–76
Plastics, benefits of, 28
Polyform Corporation, 15–16, 32, 90
Polyform polymer clay, 15–16, 32
Polymer clay artists, xi, 23
Polymer clays. *See also* Baking process;
    Brands of polymer clays; Projects using
    polymer clays
        acrylic paints on, 26
        as art form, xi
        cleaning up, 33–35
        color intensity scale for, 17
        conditioning time scale for, 17
        developments in, xi
        for faux or imitative techniques, 5, 7, 28
        makeup on, 26
        microwaving, avoiding, 15
        for millefiori technique, 5, 7
        paint on, 26
        questions about, x
        storing, 35
        tensile strength of, 16
        textures and, 23
Potions for texture, 24–26
Powders for texture, 24–26
Power tools for working with polymer
    clays, 22
Primary colors, 36–37
Professional association resources, 91
Projects
    Chocolate Sweets for the Dieter, 42–43
    Christmas Package Frame, 72–76
    Christmas Tree Box, 82–87
    Gilded Antique Frame, 56–59
    Good Morning, Glory! Garden Soap
        Dish, 66–71
    Grandma's Old-Fashioned "No-Cal"
        Sugar Cookies, 44–47
    Internet Ink Pen, 48–51
    Recycled Santa Lightbulb Ornament,
        77–81

Red-Flowered Lid, 55
    "Spicy" Jar Lids, 52–55
    Springtime Birdhouse Ornament, 60–65
PROMAT polymer clay
    baking process for, 28
    colors of, 13
    conditioning, 14–15
    described, 13
Pro tool, 20
Pyrex cake pans, for baking polymer
    clays, 28–29

Quick Tite glue, 30

Recycled Santa Lightbulb Ornament
    project, 77–81
Red-Flowered Lid project, 55
Resources
    books, xi, 29, 91–92
    companies, 89–91
    magazines, 91, 93
    online, 92
    other, 93
    professional associations, 91
    trade associations, 91
    videos, 92
Roche, Nan, xi
Rose cutters, 20
Rub 'n Buff potion, 26

Safety tips for working with polymer clays
    baking process, 15, 32
    finishes, 33
    glues, 30
    tools, 22
Sandpaper, wet and dry, 21–22
Sax Arts & Crafts, 91
Sculpey III polymer clay
    baking process for, 15, 28
    color mixing, 14, 39
    colors of, 14
    conditioning, 15
    described, 14
    finish of, 32
    Polyform polymer clay and, 15–16, 32
    predictable factors of, 14–15
Sealing finishes, 26

Secondary colors, 36–38
Shade, defined, 36
Shapes, 26–28
Soap dish, making, 66–71
Sobo glue, 31–32
Society of Craft Designers, 91
Solid Diluent softening agent, 14
"Spicy" Jar Lids project, 52–55
Spring-loaded plunger, 20
Springtime Birdhouse Ornament project,
 60–65
Steinmann, Charles (Chuck), 15
Stone colors of FIMO, 5, 11
Storage of polymer clays, 35
Super Elasticlay softening agent, 14
Super glues, 30–31
Super Sculpey polymer clay, 16

Techniques for working with polymer
 clays
   color mixing, 36-39
   marbleizing, 36
Tempered glass work surface, 18
Tensile strength chart, 16
Tertiary colors, 38
Textures
   found objects for, 24

items for creating, 23–24
polymer clays and, 23
powders and potions for, 24–26
variety of, 23
Thomas Scientific (manufacturer), 91
Tinting technique, 36
Tone, defined, 36
Tools for working with polymer
 clays, 20–24
Trade association resources, 91
Translucent formulas of FIMO, 5

Ultraglaze finish, 33

Varnishes, 32–33
Video resources, 92

Wee Folk Creations, 91
Wheat paste glue, 30
Wilton (manufacturer), 91
Work habits
   eye strain, avoiding, 19
   lighting, 19
   posture, good, 19
   tools, 20–24
   work surface, 18–19
Work surface, 18–19